VIETNAM COASTAL AND RIVERINE FORCES HANDBOOK

SGT. EDWARD M. LEONARD, USMC VIETNAM WAR COLLECTION

VIETNAM
COASTAL AND RIVERINE
FORCES
HANDBOOK

by

Barry Gregory

148

PSL

Patrick Stephens

First published in 1988

British Library Cataloguing in Publication Data

Gregory, Barry
Vietnam coastal & riverine forces.
1. Indochinese War, 1946–1954—Naval
operations   2. Vietnamese Conflict,
1961–1975—Naval operations
I. Title
959.704'345   DS553.1

ISBN 1-85260-023-3

*Patrick Stephens Limited is part of the
Thorsons Publishing Group, Wellingborough,
Northamptonshire, NN8 2RQ, England*

Printed in Great Britain by Woolnough Bookbinding Limited,
Irthlingborough, Northamptonshire

1   3   5   7   9   10   8   6   4   2

CONTENTS

ACKNOWLEDGEMENTS

The author wishes to thank the staff of the United States Navy Historical Center, Washington Navy Yard, Washington, DC 20374 and in particular Mr Ed Marolda for providing the official naval accounts and after-combat reports upon which most of the historical background to this book has been based and also the Department of the Army's *Riverine Operations*, Vietnam Studies, 1966-69, for information on the US 9th Infantry Division. My thanks also to Mr John Moore of Military Archives and Research Services (MARS) for his help in researching and acquiring the photographs; not forgetting Colonel Victor J. Croizat USMC (Retd) who first aroused my interest in the Brown Water Navy.

Barry Gregory
London, England

HISTORICAL BACKGROUND

Vietnam appears on a map of Asia as an elongated figure of eight along the eastern edge of the Indochinese peninsula. It is made up of two river basins — the Red and the Mekong — separated by a narrow chain of mountains backing on even narrower coastal plains.

The Red River delta is separated from the coastal lowlands to the south by low lying hills that also serve as the boundary between the old provinces of Tonkin and Annam. Elsewhere the delta is surrounded by rugged mountains that jut abruptly out of the alluvial plain to form the frontier shared with China and Laos.

During the nineteenth century the French had used the waterways comprising the Red, Black and Clear Rivers in the north and the Mekong, Bassac, Dong Nai, Saigon, and Van Co Rivers of Cochinchina in the south in the conquest of Indochina. Even in peacetime most of the traffic in the north of Vietnam was by waterways. In wartime, with roads and railways frequently cut by enemy action, the French estimated that 90 per cent of traffic would be by inland waterway. It is not surprising therefore that in the First Indochina War (1946-54) the French should turn to the waterways of the north for military operations.

When the French marched into Hanoi in 1946 (then the administrative capital of the whole of Indochina) Ho Chi Minh's nationalist forces were already well organized. In the riverine theatre, the French started out with craft that were available locally — native or left by the Japanese — which they modified with armour and armament. In addition, they received from the British some LCIs (landing craft, infantry) and a few LCAs (landing craft, assault) and LCTs (landing craft, tank).

Originally the responsibility of the French Army, by 1946 the French Navy had organized these craft into river flotillas that were designed for the transport of 'commandos' and river patrols. In 1947, the river flotillas were designated *Divisions navales d'assaut* (naval assault divisions) abbreviated to *dinassauts*. The divisions were initially designed to provide transport with fire support escort. In their time their composition changed according to the areas of operation. Each flotilla had from twelve to eighteen craft, ranging from LCVPs (landing craft, vehicle or personnel) to LSSLs (landing ships, support, large) and contained at least these elements:

Command and fire support	1 LCI or LSSL
Transport	1 LCT
Landing and support	1 LCU and 4 LCVPs
Patrol and liaison	1 Harbour

Each flotilla could transport and land an infantry force of

approximately battalion strength and its equipment. At first, the flotillas were very successful in delivering strikes by *coup de main* but towards the end of the campaign — as the Viet Minh massed their forces — the raiders proved less effective. However, the *dinassauts* were something new and strongly influenced the Americans in the development of the Mobile Riverine Force (Task Force 117), which was to operate in the Mekong Delta from 1967-69.

South Vietnam, formerly Cochinchina, has 3,195 miles (6,400 km) of navigable waterways. The Mekong, which is one of the world's longest rivers, rises in South Tsinghai Province in China and flows for 2,600 miles (4,183 km) through Southeast Asia into the South China Sea. The Mekong Delta extends from Saigon south and west to the Gulf of Thailand and the border with Cambodia. The Delta, its geography and climate are worth looking at in some detail since this maze of waterways was the scene of major conflict between the US and the South Vietnamese navies against the Viet Cong.

With an area of about 24,860 square miles (40,000 sq km) and an estimated eight million inhabitants, the Mekong Delta consti- tuted about one-fourth of the total land area of South Vietnam, and this flat alluvial plain created by the Mekong River and its distributaries contained about one-half of the country's population. Much of the land surface is covered by rice paddies, making the area one of the world's most productive in rice growing. It was by far the most important economic region in Vietnam.

The Delta had poor overland communications, the low, poorly drained surface being subjected to extensive and prolonged inundation. There was only one major hard surface road, Route 4 (which extended from Saigon south to Ca Mau) traversing the Delta and linking many of the larger towns; the secondary roads were poorly surfaced and in the mid-1960s had deteriorated because of lack of maintenance. In short, the road network was of little use for military action.

Any movement by road was best during the dry season — November to March — when paddies were dry and could support light tracked vehicles and artillery pieces: it was poorest during the wet season — May to October — when paddies were flooded. It was restricted all year round by the network of rivers, canals, streams and ditches. Swamps, marshes and forests bordered the sea coast.

One especially swampy area was the Rung Sat Special Zone, in the Vietnam War the only territorial command of the Vietnamese Navy. 'Rung Sat' means 'dense jungle' and well describes the extensive mangrove swamp through which passed the main ship canal that linked Saigon with the sea. The Viet Cong found the relative inaccessability of the Rung Sat, its proximity to Saigon, and

8

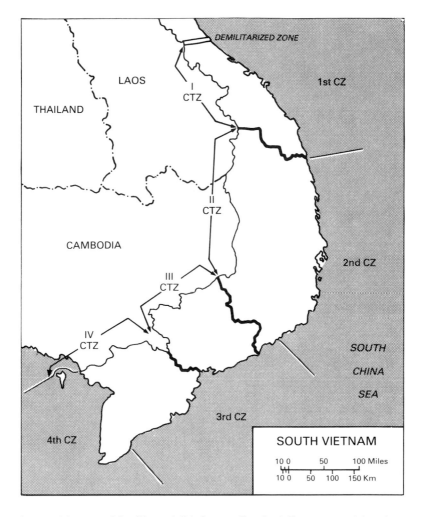

Map showing South Vietnam with Corps Tactical Zones:

- DEMILITARIZED ZONE
- LAOS
- THAILAND
- I CTZ
- 1st CZ
- II CTZ
- CAMBODIA
- 2nd CZ
- III CTZ
- IV CTZ
- SOUTH CHINA SEA
- 3rd CZ
- 4th CZ

SOUTH VIETNAM

10 0   50   100 Miles
10 0   50   100   150 Km

its position astride III and IV Corps Tactical Zones combined to make it an excellent place to maintain a large base and transient facilities.

In sharp contrast to the limited land transportation, the Delta had a highly developed inland waterway system. There is evidence that the inhabitants of the region discovered the means of improving natural drainage as long ago as 800 AD and succeeding generations have continued the work. As a result, in the mid-1960s the 1,491 miles (2,400 km) of natural, navigable waterways were supplemented by almost as many miles again of land-cut canals in varying depth, width and in good to poor condition.

From mid-May through to early October, the southwest

monsoon drenches the lowlands with rain accumulated from its passage over thousands of miles of ocean. Unleashing a torrent of savage thunderstorms in May, the weather then lapses into a monotonous pattern of afternoon showers. This rainfall and cloudiness reaches a peak in July and August, when heavy downpours often wash out the horizon and reduce the visibility to zero. The autumn transition period lasts barely a month, before the northeast monsoon season, which brings cool, dry weather from early November until March.

The wet season permits the deliberate flooding of the rice paddies, but also brings unavoidable flooding as rivers overflow their banks further restricting the cross-country traffic of military ordnance and equipment.

One third of the Delta is marsh, forest or swamp forest. In the north lies the Plain of Reeds, a flat, grassy basin. During the wet season it is inundated to a depth of 6/9 ft (2/3 m): during the dry season much of the plain dries out to the extent that large grass fires are frequent.

Riverine operations in the Delta in the Vietnam War also had to deal daily with the strong influence of sea tides. The twice-daily tidal flow influences the velocity of currents, and has an important bearing on the feasibility of navigation in many waterways. Variations in sea tides together with the complex nature of the interconnecting waterways make tidal effects exceptionally difficult to predict with confidence.

THE US SEVENTH FLEET MOVES IN

President John F. Kennedy's decision in November 1961 to expand the use of American support units in South Vietnam resulted in the US Navy's general-purpose forces offering even greater assistance. In 'limited partnership' with the South Vietnamese armed forces, the US Navy deployed major fleet units to the increasingly hostile region. Beginning in December 1961, Seventh Fleet and Vietnamese Navy units conducted combined surface and air patrols along the 17th parallel (the line of demarcation between the republics of North and South Vietnam) from the coast eastward to the Paracel Islands.

The purpose of the patrol was twofold: to train the South Vietnamese Sea Force in open-sea deployment and to determine the extent of any waterborne infiltration of munitions from North Vietnam. Aided in their surveillance mission by SP-5B Marlin seaplanes based on Taiwan, the five minesweepers of Mine sweeping Division 13 constituted the initial surface force deployed to the area but they were soon relieved by faster and more seaworthy destroyer escort ships.

A similar effort was mounted in the Gulf of Thailand, where US and South Vietnamese naval forces sought to verify the existence of communist infiltration of arms and supplies from Cambodia into the Ca Mau Peninsula and adjacent areas. Training the Vietnamese Navy in blue water surveillance operations was also a goal in this area. Destroyer escorts *Wiseman* (DE 667) and *Walton* (DE 361) initiated the combined patrol when they steamed into the Gulf of Siam on 27 February 1962. For the next three months, US ships used their radar to vector South Vietnamese patrol vessels to suspicious contacts for boarding and search.

Other Seventh Fleet ships were used to gather information on the suitability of South Vietnamese beaches for amphibious landings. During January 1962 *Cook* (APD 130) steamed along the South Vietnamese coast conducting beach surveys from Quang Tai in the north to Vung Tau in the south. The following year, in February and March, *Weiss* (APD 135) made a similar transit along the South Vietnamese littoral. On several occasions, shore parties from the ship were fired on by the Viet Cong.

Despite the infusion of material aid, advisory assistance, and direct support by American military, it became abundantly clear during 1964 that the land-based counter–insurgency struggle against the Viet Cong in South Vietnam was failing. Inevitably the US Navy became involved in a broader counter–insurgency effort. One of the initial measures, a series of sabotage operations begun in February 1964 under Operation Plan 34A, was conducted in

North Vietnam by South Vietnamese 'frogmen' and boat crews using American PTF motor torpedo boats.

During 31 July and 1 August 1964 the US destroyer *Maddox* (DD 731) was cruising uneventfully along a pre-designated track in international waters off the North Vietnamese coast. Until, that is, in the early hours of 2 August, Captain John S. Herrick learned from intelligence that North Vietnamese naval forces planned to attack his vessel. This impending action was clearly meant as a reprisal for the striking of targets on Hon Me and Hon Niea islands lying a short distance off the coast of North Vietnam by four South Vietnamese Swift boats. These boats had attempted to put commandos ashore on Hon Me but had withdrawn after strong resistance. The order had been given to bombard targets in North Vietnam for the first time and the Swifts had opened up with machine-gun and cannon fire on the two islands.

Directed to continue his patrol, the *Maddox* reached a point east of Thanh Hoa in the Gulf of Tonkin about 10.45 hours (local time). Two hours later, lookouts and radars picked up North Vietnamese naval craft north of Hon Me. Later identified as three P-4 motor torpedo boats in column, *Maddox* (after sending warning shots) opened fire with her 5-in/.38 calibre guns. For the next twenty minutes the destroyer manoeuvred to avoid torpedos and engaged the PTs with gunfire. Passing astern of the destroyer, all of the P-4s were hit. As *Maddox*, struck by only one 14.5 mm round, headed out to sea, four F-8 Crusader naval aircraft from the carrier USS *Ticonderoga* appeared and attacked the retreating North Vietnamese craft. One of the P-4s slowed by the damage, was set on fire and sank. This short, sharp naval action was the first round in a new confrontation with North Vietnam.

Within hours of the engagement, *Maddox*, now accompanied by *Turner Joy* (DD 951) resumed the interrupted patrol in international waters around Hon Me. In the meantime the Swifts also returned to operations as the 34A maritime force got underway. Three South Vietnamese-crewed Swifts reached their operating area off Cape Doc around midnight on 3 August. The motor torpedo boats shelled a radar facility at Vinh Son and a security post on the south bank of the Ron River. Their mission accomplished, the boats withdrew and made for Danang.

The raid caused the North Vietnamese forces to react once again. At 20.41, 4 August the *Maddox* and *Turner Joy* picked up fast approaching contacts on their radars. At 22.39 one of the P-4 motor torpedo boats closed to 7,000 yards (6,400 m) and Captain Herrick ordered the *Turner Joy* to open fire. For the next two hours the American destroyers, covered overhead by carrier aircraft, evaded several torpedos and fired on the attacking craft, successfully chasing them off. Later *Maddox* and *Turner Joy* returned to the *Ticonderoga* Carrier Task Group steaming around the entrance to the Tonkin gulf.

On 7 August 1964, the Tonkin Gulf Resolution, proposed by the Johnson Adminstration, was passed unanimously by the House of Representatives and approved in the Senate by an 88 to 2 margin. Prompted by the above events in the Gulf of Tonkin, this measure authorized the President to use US armed forces to assist in the defence of the non-communist nations of Southeast Asia. This resolution served as the legal basis for the armed support provided by the United States to South Vietnam throughout the Vietnam War.

NAVAL COMMAND IN SOUTHEAST ASIA

As the US Navy entered heavy combat in Southeast Asia during the years from 1965 to 1968, a chain of command evolved which reflected the complex character of the war. In theory, Commander-in-Chief, Pacific (CINCPAC) was the commander of all American forces in Asia, including those assigned to Commander US Military Assistance Command, Vietnam (COMUSMACV). However, as the conflict in South Vietnam intensified, COMUSMACV came to exert the greatest influence over in-country operations. At the same time, the need to control and coordinate the bombing campaign in North Vietnam and Laos, the massive transpacific logistic effort, and other American military activities in the Far East required CINCPAC's full attention.

The US Pacific Fleet was the naval component of the Pacific Command and as such directed the Navy's activities in that ocean. Subordinate to Commander-in-Chief US Pacific Fleet (CINC-PACFLT) was the Commander Seventh Fleet, who conducted those naval operations in Southeast Asia primarily external to South Vietnam. The fleet's Attack Carrier Striking Force (Task Force 77) mounted the aerial interdiction campaign in Laos and North Vietnam from the South China Sea. Commander Seventh Fleet's cruiser and destroyer units hunted the enemy's logistic craft along the North Vietnamese coast, bombarded targets ashore, and provided naval gunfire support to allied forces in South Vietnam. The Amphibious Force (Task Force 76) and its attached Marine units conducted numerous over-the-beach and helicopter landings in search of the elusive Viet Cong in South Vietnam. The Mobile Logistic Support Force (part of Task Force 77) laboured to keep the fleet's combatants on station and engaged with the enemy.

Although the fleet's Attack Carrier Striking Force (Task Force 77) does not fall within the scope of this book brief reference should be made to its important role in the Vietnam War. From the South China Sea, Task Force 77 mounted the 'Rolling Thunder' bombing and 'Blue Tree' tactical reconnaissance operations in North Vietnam; the 'Barrel Roll', 'Steel Tiger', and 'Tiger Hound' bombing and 'Yankee Team' reconnaissance efforts in Laos; and the ground support mission in South Vietnam. Except during the period 1965 and 1966 when the aircraft carrier supporting operations in the South sailed at Dixie Station, the carrier task force was deployed at Yankee Station (after April 1966 at 17° 30′N 108° 30′E).

Prior to August 1966, two or three carriers operated in Task Force 77, but after that date the number was often three or four. On each ship a carrier wing controlled between 70 and 100 aircraft,

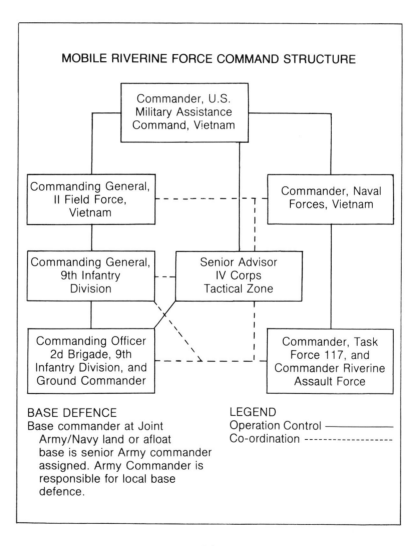

MOBILE RIVERINE FORCE COMMAND STRUCTURE

Commander, U.S. Military Assistance Command, Vietnam

Commanding General, II Field Force, Vietnam

Commander, Naval Forces, Vietnam

Commanding General, 9th Infantry Division

Senior Advisor IV Corps Tactical Zone

Commanding Officer 2d Brigade, 9th Infantry Division, and Ground Commander

Commander, Task Force 117, and Commander Riverine Assault Force

BASE DEFENCE
Base commander at Joint Army/Navy land or afloat base is senior Army commander assigned. Army Commander is responsible for local base defence.

LEGEND
Operation Control ——————
Co-ordination ------------------

usually grouped in two fighter and three attack squadrons and smaller detachments. However, the number depended on the size and class of the carriers, which varied from the large-deck 'Enterprise' (CVAN 65) and 'Forrestal' (CVA 59) class ships of 90,970/79,250 tons to the 33,000-ton World War 2 'Hancock' class ships.

The Navy's mainline strike aircraft included the A-4 Skyhawk, propeller-driven A-1 Skyraider, A-7 Corsair II, and all-weather, day-night A-6 Intruder for strike operations. The workhorse F-4 Phantom II, in addition to its attack role, flew in the fighter escort role, as did the F-8 Crusader.

COASTAL INTERDICTION: TASK FORCE 115 (1965-73)

The Coastal Surveillance Force (Task Force 115) was responsible for halting Communist infiltration of men and arms into South Vietnam by sea. Operation 'Market Time' conducted by Task Force 115 was organized around eight (later nine) patrol sectors covering the 120-mile (193 km) South Vietnamese coast from the 17th parallel to the Cambodian border and extending 40 miles (64 km) out to sea. Within these areas, surface search was carried out by ships and craft of the US Navy, the US Coast Guard, and the South Vietnamese Navy. American aircraft operating from ships offshore and from bases in South Vietnam, Thailand and the Philippines carried out aerial surveillance of the 'Market Time' area.

Later in the war, the task of preventing seaborne infiltration was divided into three zones: an aerial sector farthest out to sea; an outer, surface barrier; patrolled by the large US ships (employed principally on coastal bombardment); and a shallow-water barrier patrolled by US and South Vietnamese boats and Coastal Force junks. An additional screen was created after April 1966 when Mobile Inshore Undersea Warfare Surveillance Group 1, Western Pacific Detachment, units (IUVU) were deployed in operation 'Stable Door', to provide harbour defence and patrol at key South Vietnamese ports.

The years 1965-68 witnessed a great increase in 'Market Time' resources and the full development of patrol tactics and operating procedures. During the first months of the patrol in 1965 an average of fifteen destroyers and minesweepers (MSO or MSC) steamed off South Vietnam with at least one ship assigned to each of the sectors.

DESTROYERS

Typical of US destroyers deployed in South Vietnam waters in the early years of the conflict were the *Maddox* and *Turner Joy*.

'Allen M. Sumner' class

Of World War 2 origin, the 'Allen M. Sumner' class was modified three times before the *Maddox* saw service in Southeast Asian waters. The *Maddox* is described here as she was on arrival at Pearl Harbor en route for Vietnam, 9 March 1964.

Displacement 2,200 (standard) tons, 3,320 full load **Length** 376.5 ft (114 m) **Beam** 40.9 ft (12 m) **Draft** 19 ft (6 m) **Guns** six 5-in/.38 calibre dual

Maddox *(DD 731) a famous representative of the 'Allen M. Sumner'*
destroyer (DD) class.

purpose (twin); four 3-in/.50 calibre AA (twin) **ASW weapons** two fixed
hedgehogs, depth charges; two triple torpedo launchers (Mk 32) **Main
engines** two geared turbines 60,000 shp, two shafts, four boilers **Speed**
34 knots **Complement** 274 (14 officers, 260 enlisted men).

'Forrest Sherman' class

The *Turner Joy* was one of the first US destroyers of post World
War 2 design and construction.

Displacement 2,850 (standard) tons, 4,050 full load **Length** 418 ft (127
m) **Beam** 45 ft (14 m) **Draft** 20 ft (6 m) **Missiles** one single surface-to-air
launcher **Guns** (ASW mod) two 5-in/.54 calibre dual purpose, two
5-in/.54 calibre dual purpose, two 5-in/.50 calibre AA (twin) **ASW
Weapons** one ARSOC eight-tube launcher, two triple torpedo launchers
(Mk 32), two hedgehogs, depth charges, two triple torpedo launchers (Mk
32) **Main engines** two geared turbines (General Electric), 70,000 shp,
two shafts, four Babcock & Wheeler boilers **Speed** 33 knots,
Complement 292 (17 officers and 275 enlisted men).

Turner Joy *(DD 951)* *'Forrest Sherman' guided missile destroyer (DD) class.*

MINESWEEPERS

Forming some of the earliest 'Market Time' patrols ocean minesweepers (MSO) saw the war through to the last as the final provision of the American ceasefire agreement signed in Paris on 27 January 1973 required MSOs escorted by destroyers to put to sea to sweep anchorage areas off the Vietnam coast near Haiphong.

'Bluebird' class

Numerous coastal minesweepers were produced in shipyards in the USA and supplied to NATO and non-aligned countries. MSC 281 (*Ham Tu II* - HQ 114), MSC 282 (*Chu O'ng - Du 'O' Ng II* - HQ 115) and MSC 283 (*Bach Dang II* - HQ 116) of the non-magnetic, 'Bluebird' class, of wooden construction were supplied to the South Vietnamese Navy via the French Navy on 11 February 1954.

Displacement 320 (standard) tons, 370 full load **Length** 144 ft (44 m) **Beam** 28 ft (9 m) **Draft** 9 ft (2.7 m) **Guns** one 20 mm AA **Main engines** two diesels, 1,200 bhp **Speed** 13 knots **Complement** 45 (4 officers and 41 enlisted men).

FAST PATROL BOATS

Two types of fast patrol boats were used on clandestine missions in Southeast Asia — the 'Nasty' class (two types) and the smaller, slower 'Swift' class.

'Nasty' class

When Viet Cong activity in South Vietnam was first demonstrated on any scale, the South Vietnamese Navy despatched 'Nastys' with commandos on board to attack supply centres in North Vietnam. PTF 3-16 of the 'Nasty' type were built by Boatservice Ltd, A/S of Handel Norway, to the same design as the Norwegian Navy's 'Tjeld' class torpedo boats. Delivery to the USA of these eight craft had been completed by September 1964. Hulls were made of two layers of mahogany which sandwiched a layer of fibreglass.

Displacement 69 (standard) tons, 64 light, 76 full load **Length** 80.3 ft (24 m) **Beam** 24.5 ft (7 m) **Draft** 6.8 ft (2 m) **Guns** (varied) 40 mm single, two 20 mm single **Main engines** two diesels (Napier-Deltic) 6,200 shp, two shafts **Speed** 45 knots **Complement** 19 (3 officers and 16 enlisted men).

PTF 17-26 were built in the USA, their design based on the 'Nasty' type boats built in Norway.

Displacement 69 (standard) tons, 64 light, 76 full load **Length** 80.3 ft (24 m) **Beam** 25.5 ft (8 m) **Draft** 6.8 ft (2 m) **Guns** (varied) one 81 mm mortar, one 40 mm, two 20 mm (single), one .50 calibre MG (mounted over mortar) **Main engines** two diesels (Napier-Deltic), 6,200 shp, two shafts **Speed** 45 knots **Complement** 19 (3 officers and 16 enlisted men).

Fast Patrol Boat (PTF): 'Nasty' type.

Above and top *Fast patrol boat (PTF): 'New Construction' type.*
Two views of PTF-23 in Vietnam coastal waters in 1970.

'Swift' class

In order to augment the patrol close inshore, the US Navy acquired
104 'Swift' Mk I boats and then eight similar MK IIs. The 'Swift'
type was adapted from the all-metal crew boat which was used to
support off-shore drilling rigs in the Gulf of Mexico. 'Swift' boat Mk
Is were built by Stewart Seacraft Inc, Berwick, Louisiana, USA,
1965-66. The 'Swifts' were the mainstay of the US Coastal
Surveillance Force. Controlled by Boat Squadron 1 (later Coastal
Squadron 1), Subordinate Boat Divisions 101, 102, 103, 104 and
105 (designated Coastal Divisions 11, 12, 13, 14 and 15 on 1
January 1967) were established at An Thoi, Danang, Cat Lo, Cam
Ranh Bay, and Qui Nonh respectively. An additional 'Swift' boat

Swift boats transit a narrow canal during Operation 'Slingshot'.

unit, Coastal Division 16, was activated at Chu Lai in June 1967.

In addition to constant coastal interdiction assignments, the 'Swift' boats inserted the SEAL US Navy commandos on beaches along the coast and on the banks of the River Mekong and the Delta where the PCFs were also used as interceptors.

Displacement PCFs 1-104 series 22.5 tons full load **Length** 50 ft (15 m) **Beam** 13 ft (4 m) **Draft** 3.5 ft (1 m) **Guns** one 81 mm mortar, three .50 calibre MG (twin mounted atop pilot house and single MG mounted over

A boatswain's mate aboard a Swift boat peppers an enemy position with an M-60 machine gun. This PCF is patrolling a river in the Lower Ca Mau peninsula.

Above *PCF 9 manoeuvres around an enemy barrier during a patrol on the Duong Keo River and the Ca Mau peninsula.*

Below *Swift boats beach to disembark Vietnamese marines on a sweep operation along a lower Ca Mau peninsula river.*

PCF 71 conducts a lone patrol through a narrow canal, Operation 'Slingshot'.

mortar) **Main engines** two geared diesels (General Motors) 960 shp, two shafts **Speed** 28 knots (maximum) **Complement** 6 (1 officer and 5 enlisted men) three crews were provided for every two boats in action in the Vietnam War.

US Coast Guard cutters

A number of US Coast Guard cutters supplemented US Navy forces in the Vietnam War. These vessels remained units of the US Coast Guard, but were under the operational direction of the Commander US Naval Forces Vietnam. Both 82 ft (25 m) and high endurance cutters joined in the 'Market Time' assignment to halt Communist infiltration of men and supplies from North into South Vietnam by sea.

The 82 ft (25 m) cutters were designed and built by the US Coast Guard for law enforcement, search and rescue roles. The WPB were steel hulled and the unmanned engine room was controlled from the bridge. The craft were equipped with power steering and their interiors were air conditioned. Those cutters on Vietnam service were assigned to Coast Guard Squadron One and based at An Thoi, Danang and Cat Lo.

Displacement 64 (standard) tons, 67 full load **Length** 82 ft (25 m) **Beam** 17.2 ft (3.3 m) **Draft** 5.8 ft (2 m) **Guns** one 20 mm/.50 calibre MG, two to four .50 calibre MG or one 20mm **Main engines** two diesels, 12 bhp, two shafts **Speed** 22.9 knots **Complement** 8 to 10 men.

Above and top Bibb *(WHEC 31) and* Campbell *(WHEC 32) high endurance cutters of the 'Campbell' (327) class.*

The continuing demand for 'Market Time' vessels resulted in the deployment to South Vietnam, during 1967 and 1968, of 15 US Coast Guard high endurance cutters (WHEC). Operating under Coast Guard Squadron Three, the WHECs were equipped with search radars and carried considerable firepower.

Displacement 2,216 (standard) tons, 2,414 full load **Length** 327 ft (99 m) **Beam** 41 ft (12 m) **Draft** 15 ft (4.5 m) **Guns** one 5-in/.38 calibre dual purpose, six .50 calibre MG, two 81 mm mortars **A/S weapons** two triple torpedo launchers (Mk 32) hedgehog **Main engines** two Westinghouse geared turbines, 6,200 shp, two shafts, two boilers (Babcock & Wilcox) **Speed** 19.8 knots **Complement** 144 (13 officers and 131 enlisted men).

RADAR PICKET SHIPS

Thirty-six 'Edsall' class destroyers were converted to radar picket ships between 1951 and 1958 and redesignated 'DER'. DERs replaced the original fifteen destroyers (DE) on 'Market Time' patrol. When the coastal interdiction programme commenced in 1965, operations met with great success but the situation had begun to deteriorate until on the evening of 31 December 1965, *Hissem* (DER 400) detected a small trawler heading for the shore of the Ca Mau Peninsula. The ship, a trawler, realizing that it had been observed and flying a foreign flag, turned around and headed north aborting the mission. The first concrete success of the new programme occurred in May 1966 when 'Market Time' forces intercepted and destroyed another infiltrating trawler on the coast of An Xuyen Province. The cargo, which was recovered, consisted of mortar and small arms ammunition manufactured in a communist country during 1965.

Although eleven of the original converted destroyers were allocated to the US Coast Guard service, most of the remainder served 'Market Time' in the South China Sea and the Gulf of Tonkin.

Displacement 1,590 (standard) tons, 1,850 full load **Length** 306 ft (93 m) **Beam** 36.6 ft (11 m) **Draft** 14 ft (4.25 m) **Guns** two 3-in/.50 calibre AA **ASW weapons** two triple torpedo launchers (Mk 32) in active ships, one trainable hedgehog depth charge **Main engines** four diesels (Fairbanks Morse), 6,000 shp, two shafts **Speed** 21 knots **Complement** 169 (19 officers and 150 enlisted men).

PATROL GUNBOATS
'Ashville' class

The 'Ashville' class patrol gunboats (PG) commissioned between 1966 and 1970 were at the time the largest patrol-type craft built by the US Navy since World War 2 and the first US Navy ships equipped with gas-turbine propulsion. They were designed to perform coastal patrol, blockade surveillance, perimeter defence, and support missions. There was no anti-submarine capability. The newly built 'Ashville' class made its first appearance in Southeast Asia with the deployment of *Gallup* (PG 85) which was ordered and launched in less than five months, and the establishment of Coastal Squadron Three (part of Task Force 77). Coastal Flotilla 1 was then created to operate the ship and its sisters.

Displacement 225 (standard) tons, 240 full load **Length** 164.5 ft (50 m) **Beam** 23.8 ft (7 m) **Draft** 9.5 ft (3 m) **Guns** one 3-in/.50 calibre (forward)

one 40 mm (aft) **Main engines** one gas turbine (General Electric), 13,300 shp, two shafts **Speed** 40+ knots **Complement** 24 (3 officers, 21 enlisted men).

HYDROFOIL PATROL GUNBOATS

Two hydrofoil patrol gunboats, the *Tucumcari* (PGH 1) and the *Flagstaff* (PGH 2), were assigned to Task Force 115 later in the war. These vessels were soon judged to be unsuited to patrol in

Left Ashville *(PG 84),* **below left** Gallup *(PG 85) and* **bottom left** Welch *(PG 93), patrol gunboats (PG) of the 'Ashville' class.*

Below and bottom The Tucumcari *(PGH 2) hydrofoil gunboat.*

the rough seas of Vietnam and mechanically too complex for the repair facilities in the combat theatre.

'Tucumcari' class

The *Tucumcari* was built by the Boeing Company in Seattle, Washington and the hull was fabricated by Gunderson Brothers of Portland, Oregon. The vessel had a canard foil configuration with approximately 30 per cent of the boat's weight supported by the forward foil and 70 per cent by the aft set of foils. The forward foil assembly provided steering by means of rotating the strut about its vertical axis. The foil-borne operation was automatic with a wave height sensing system to maintain the hull clear of the sea. The foils were fully retractable for hull-borne operations. The hull was of aluminium construction.

During the foil-borne operation the craft's gas turbine drove a water-jet pump instead of a propeller. Water was taken in from the sea through the openings in the main pods and carried in ducts within the foil struts to the pump inlet. The water — at the rate of approximately 27,000 gallons (100 tons) per minute — was then pumped out through the nozzles under the craft's stern to obtain thrust. Hull-borne operation was by means of a diesel-driven water-jet pump.

Displacement 58 tons **Length** 71.8 ft (22 m) **Beam** 19.5 ft (6 m) **Draft** 4.5 ft (1.3 m) (hull-borne) **Guns** one 40 mm, four 20 mm calibre MG (twin), one 81 mm mortar **Main engines** foil-borne: one gas turbine (Proteus), 3,100 hp water jet propulsion (hull-borne) one diesel (General Motors), 150 shp water-jet propulsion **Speed** 40+ knots **Complement** 13 (1 officer and 12 enlisted men).

'Flagstaff' class

The *Flagstaff* was the competitive prototype evaluated with the *Tucumcari*. Built by Grumman Aircraft Corporation in Stuart, Florida, this hydrofoil was laid down on 15 July 1966, launched on 9 January 1968, and placed in service in July 1968. The *Flagstaff* had a conventional foil arrangement with 70 per cent of the craft's weight supported by the forward set of foils and 30 per cent of the weight supported by the stern foils. Steering was accomplished by movement of the stern strut about its vertical axis. Foil-borne operation was automatically controlled by a wave-height sensing system. The foils were fully retractable for hull-borne operations. The hull was of aluminium construction.

During foil-borne operations the propeller was driven by a geared transmission system contained in the tail-strut and in the

The Flagstaff *(PGH 2) hydrofoil gunboat.*

pod located at the strut-foil connection. During hull-borne operations two diesel engines drove a water-jet propulsion system. Water entered the pump inlets through openings in the hull and the thrust was exerted by water flow through nozzles in the transom. Steering in the hull-borne mode was by deflection vanes in the water stream.

Displacement 57 tons **Length** 74.4 ft (23 m) **Beam** 21.4 ft (6.5 m) **Draft** 4.2 ft (1.2 m) hull-borne **Guns** one 40 mm, four .50 calibre MG (twin), one 81 mm mortar **Main engines** (foil-borne) one gas turbine (Rolls Royce), 2,600 hp, controllable pitch propeller; (hull-borne) two diesels (General Motors), 300 hp, water jet propulsion **Speed** 40+ knots **Complement** 13 (1 officer and 12 enlisted men).

TASK FORCE 115 AERIAL SURVEILLANCE

The aerial surveillance of South Vietnamese coastal waters was conducted by various aircraft from different locations. For a brief time in 1965 A-1 Skyraiders based on carriers at Dixie Station flew along the Annam coast. This mission was shared and then taken over by a patrol squadron based at Sangley Point in the Philippines equipped with the advanced P-3 Orion aircraft. Throughout this period five to seven P-2 Neptunes stationed at Tan Son Nhut near Saigon ranged up and down the South Vietnamese littoral along designated patrol tracks. In addition, from May 1965 to April 1967 P-5 Marlin seaplanes operated from seaplane tenders. *Carrituck* (AV 7) and *Salisbury Sound* (AV 13), periodically anchored at Condore and Cham islands and at Cam Ranh Bay. To compensate for the withdrawal of the seaplanes in March 1967, a squadron of twelve P-2s was stationed ashore at Cam Ranh Bay and a

29

A Neptune surveillance aircraft takes a look at a coastal junk sailing in the South China Sea.

detachment of P-3s began coverage of the Gulf of Siam from Utapao in Thailand. On an intermittent basis, American L-19 observation aircraft and South Vietnamese C-47s conducted surveillance of several critical coastal sectors.

P2 Neptune

The first US Navy contract for the Neptune was placed in April 1944 and several versions have appeared over the years. In Vietnam the aircraft was usually equipped for the maritime reconnaissance bomber role. The powerplant consisted of two Wright R-3350 eighteen-cylinder two-row air-cooled engines driving the Hamilton Standard Hydromatic constant speed airscrews.

All P-2E, P-2G and P-2H aircraft also had two Westinghouse J34 turbojets (each 3,400 lb/1,540 kg) in underwing pods. The fuel tanks were self-sealing with nylon plastic casing. The maximum range was 3,685 miles (5,929 km) and the crew up to seven men.

P3A Orion

The P3A Orion, the military version of the four-turboprop Electra civil airliner which was flying the world air routes in the early 1960s, was the initial production version for the US Navy. Powered by four 4,500 eshp (with water injection) Allison T56-A-LOW turboprop engines, the P-3B was equipped with 4,910 eshp Allison T-56-A-A-14 turboprop engines, which did not need water alcohol injection. The P-3C, advanced version for the US Navy, was fitted with the A-New system of sensors and control equipment, built

Above *A Lockheed 185 Orion (P-3B), US Navy designation P-3 (formerly P3V-1).*

Below and bottom *Two views of the Marlin flying boat, on patrol and being serviced in a special rubber U dock alongside USS* Ashland.

around a Univac digital computer which permitted retrieval, transmission and display of tactical data, with great speed and accuracy. First flight of the P-3C was made on 18 October 1968 and it entered service in 1969. The maximum range was 4,993 miles (8,033 km) and the crew, twelve men.

P5M Marlin

The P5M was the first twin-engine flying boat to be developed for the US Navy for anti-submarine warfare after World War 2. Two versions existed: P5M-1 and P5M-2. The powerplant consisted of two 3,250 hp Wright R-3350-36WA or 3,400 hp R-3350-32WD or R-3350-32WA, turbo compound engines with Hamilton standard airscrews. Fuel tanks in the centre wing section were of self-sealing Mareng type. Tanks in the hull and two auxiliary tanks outboard of service tanks, one in each wing panel, were non-self-sealing. Two droppable tanks could be installed, one in each nacelle bomb bay. The range (ASW mission) was 2,050 miles (3,298 km); ferry range 3,100 miles (4,988 km). The crew usually constituted 8 men.

SEAPLANE TENDERS

Launched during the Second World War, two seaplane tenders, the *Carrituck* and *Salisbury Sound*, were recommissioned for service in the Vietnam War to support P5M Marlin patrol aircraft.

The Askari *(APL 30) (ex LST 1131) landing craft repair ship (converted LST type).*

Displacement 9,106 (standard) tons, 15,092 full load **Length** 540.4 ft (164 m) **Beam** 69.2 ft (21 m) **Draft** 26 ft (8 m) **Guns** four 5-in/.38 calibre DP **Main engines** geared turbines (Parsons in *Carrituck*, Allis Chalmers in *Salisbury Sound*) of 12,000 shp, two shafts, four Babcock & Wilcox boilers **Speed** 19.2 knots **Complement** approximately 555 (30 officers and 525 men).

BASE SHIPS

Maintenance and logistic support for 'Market Time' and the river assault craft, were provided by landing craft ships (ARL) and barracks craft (APL). Both the ARLs and APLs were converted LSIs. (For the APLs see section in this book on Task Force 117.)

The *Askari, Indra. Satyr* and *Sphinx* were activated for service in Vietnam.

Displacement 1,625 (light) tons, 4,100 full load **Length** 328 ft (100 m) **Beam** 50 ft (15 m) **Draft** 11 ft (3.3 m) **Guns** eight 40 mm AA (quad) **Main engines** diesel (General Motors), 1,800 bhp, two shafts **Speed** 11.6 knots **Complement** 251 to 286.

THE VIETNAMESE NAVY AND THE COASTAL PATROL

THE FRENCH CONNECTION

The Vietnamese armed forces were originally of French creation. Although conceived during the Indochina War in 1950, the first unit of the navy did not appear until 1953. Some progress and growth followed, but it was slow. From the first it was difficult to find men with the necessary skills. Perhaps more serious was its position far down in the Vietnamese Armed Forces hierarchy and its lack of strong leadership. Together, these factors served to keep the Navy's performance 'marginal'.

In the French fight against the Viet Minh the main naval effort had been on the northern rivers, principally the Red River. The Vietnamese river assault groups, however, the *dinassauts* as they were to be called, were actually under the control of the army. Only the sea force remained firmly under navy control and even then, the coastal surveillance mission was shared with the junk force, a paramilitary organization.

The French were compelled at first to make use of whatever boats were available for riverine operations. Later, they produced a type of 36 ft (11 m) patrol boat called the STCAN/FOM. The major boats used throughout the Indochina War, however, remained the British and American landings ships and craft produced in large quantities during World War 2.

THE 'INTER-WAR' YEARS

When Vietnam was divided into two republics after the Geneva Accords in 1954, South Vietnam inherited a large batch of boats formerly controlled by the French. In 1956, the junk force was augmented by fifty civilian-manned junks for patrolling close inshore off I Corps zone just below the 17th parallel and this militia was implemented in 1960 with approximately eighty further junks.

Modest repair facilities at Rach Gia, Cat Lo, Nha Trang, Qui Nonh and Danang were established and a mixed force comprising 84 command junks, 140 motor junks and 320 sailing junks was established in 1963. There were, however, a number of problems associated with this effort. The foremost of these was the recruitment of local personnel to man the boats and operate repair facilities.

In 1964 the efficiency of the junk force was increased when a new Japanese-American motor-junk, the *Yabuta,* joined the fleet. In an attempt to solve the personnel problem the junk force was integrated into the Vietnamese Navy in July 1965. This did not help

Above right *Another suspicious fishing boat is searched by South Vietnamese naval personnel, 1966.*

Above left *US Navy advisers and South Vietnamese sailors keep their guns ready while a crewman checks identification papers aboard a civilian sampan, during a routine junk patrol in the South China Sea in 1967.*

as much as was hoped and personnel as well as base defence problems continued to plague the newly designated Coast Force.

As constituted then in the mid-1960s, the coastal force consisted of 28 coastal groups located at 22 bases: four of these had two or three coastal groups to facilitate base defence. Each group included from 9 to 24 junks. Those operating from Vung Tau usually included three command junks, three motor-sail junks, sixteen sail-only junks and two Yabuta junks.

Coastal groups operating south of Vung Tau to Long Phu had three command junks and six motor-sail junks each. Coastal groups operating south of Long Phu to the Gulf of Thailand, where winds are unpredictable, had three command junks and seventeen motor-only junks. The Coastal Force at this time included some 4,000 Vietnamese personnel, with more than ninety US Navy advisers.

The US Navy adviser to Coastal Group (CG) 25 at Han Choi included the following remarks in his evaluation for November 1965:

'Patrol effectiveness was also restricted by extremely bad weather . . . there are certain times during the monsoon when a junk is not an adequate vessel in which to patrol. Normally CG attempts to have at least three motorized junks patrolling their area at night . . . the night patrols vary from 10-18 hours . . . The base has eight motorized junks with an average of two in the repair facility and an

Above *A commandament of a riverine assault group moves along a narrow canal in the Mekong Delta, 1966. An American adviser is seen on the right.*

Below *South Vietnamese sailors fire a 81 mm mortar aboard a former French commandament armoured assault vessel in 1966.*

Crewmen of the Vietnamese Junk Force search a Viet Cong fishing boat for arms and contraband, in 1962.

average of one at Nhatrang for supplies (we transport 85% . . . of our supplies) and an average of three on a night patrol, this leaves an average of one junk for day patrol . . .'

The Vietnamese Navy, which grew from a force of 8,242 men, 44 ships, and 200 other vessels in early 1965 to one of 17,574 personnel, 65 ships, 300 junks, and 290 other craft in mid-1968, underwent several organizational changes as well. In April 1965 the Joint General Staff decided that the Vietnamese Marine Corps would be a separate service within the armed forces. In addition the I, II, III and IV Naval Zones were redesignated Coastal Zones and the newly created III and IV Riverine Areas placed under the operational control of the army commanders of the I, II, III and IV Corps Tactical Zones. The swampland of the Rung Sat remained the Navy's charge. With the exception therefore of the ships steaming outside territorial waters, all the Navy's combat forces remained under army direction.

Another significant reorganization occurred in July 1965 when the 3,500-man, paramilitary Coastal Force was formally integrated with the Navy. Thereafter the command's divisions and the old coastal district designations were dropped as the coastal zones became operational sectors. In a similar move, in October the following year, the Vietnamese Navy was assigned administrative responsibility for the headquarters and training centre of the

An American naval officer, boatswain's mate, and a South Vietnamese naval officer scrutinize the manifest of a junk for Viet Cong soldiers disguised as civilians.

paramilitary Regional Force Boat Companies and maintenance responsibility for the 192 landing craft, vehicles and personnel (LCVP) divided between the 24 boat units in the III and IV Riverine Areas.

THE VIETNAMESE NAVY GOES TO WAR

On 1 January 1966, the Sea Force was renamed the Fleet Command and reorganized along functional lines. Flotilla 1, comprising the submarine chasers (PG) and escorts in Squadron II, the motor gunboats in Squadron 13, the large support landing ships (LSSL) in Squadron 15, and the minesweepers in Squadron 17 were responsible for sea patrol, inshore patrol, river patrol and minesweeping duties, respectively. Flotilla II, which consisted of the Vietnamese Navy's landing ships and craft, coastal oilers, and other vessels providing for logistic support, controlled Squadrons 22 and 24.

The primary mission of the Vietnamese Coastal Force, from its creation in 1960, was to curtail seaborne infiltration and conduct inshore patrols. However, the great success of American operations in the outer 'Market Time' sectors and the absence of real co-ordination between the naval services, because of communications and language problems discouraged Vietnamese initiative during this period. While the junk force stopped and searched hundreds of thousands of coastal craft fewer than 50 per cent of the patrol units were on station at any one time, and rarely at night. Even so the coastal groups destroyed a number of junks, sampans and other craft carrying munitions and enemy personnel and contributed to the general deterrence role of the 'Market Time' force. Coastal Force devoted most attention to amphibious raids, patrols of shallow inlets and river mouths, troop lifts and provided blocking support for allied ground sweeps.

The inshore and riverine patrols were nevertheless costly. Viet Cong mines in late 1966 caused the loss of an LSSL, damage to a large infantry landing ship (LSIL) and a utility landing craft (LCU). The VC mines also took their toll of the Command's MLMS fleet, which worked to keep open the shipping channel to Saigon. In August 1966 and again in January 1967, MLMS ships were sunk by mines in the Rung Sat Special Zone. The logistic flotilla charged with supplying South Vietnamese bases throughout the country, transported 4,000 tons of cargo and 5,000 passengers in 1966, but only 3,000 tons of cargo and 3,000 passengers the following year. Little improvement was made in 1968. North Vietnam naval frogmen were known to operate in the Mekong Delta against the barracks ships but registered no success.

South Vietnamese blue water sailors did, however, work with their American naval minders to rectify problems and increase operational efficiency. By the late 1960s the inshore waters and rivers were more secure than they had ever been. Further, on 15 May 1967, Fleet Command units began to take over sectors of the 'Market Time' outer barrier from US ships and by the end of the year vessels were stationed in each of the coastal zones. Thus despite its deficiencies, Fleet Command continued to develop its seagoing potential.

'VIETNAMIZATION'

The South Vietnam fleet in 1969 when American forces were in the process of being wound down in Vietnam, comprised the following boats.

Ngoc Hoi *(PCE 12), the former USS* Brattleboro *(PCE 852).*

Patrol vessels

Tuy Dong	HQ 04	*Van Don*	HQ 06

Displacement 280 (standard) tons, 380 normal, 450 full load **Length** 173.7 ft (53 m) **Beam** 23 ft (7 m) **Draft** 10.8 ft (3.2 m) **Guns** one 3 in DP, one 40 mm, four 20 mm AA **A/S weapons** two DC, two RL **Main engines** diesel, 280 bhp, two shafts **Speed** 19 knots **Complement** 60 (6 officers and 54 men)

Motor gunboats

Dinh Hai	HQ 610	*May Rut*	HQ 606
Hoa Lu	HQ 608	*Minh Hao*	HQ 602
Keo Ngua	HQ 604	*Noun Dhu*	HQ 607
Kien Vong	HQ 603	*Phu Du*	HQ 600
Thai Binh	HQ 612	*To Yen*	HQ 609
Thi Tu	HQ 613	*Truong Sa*	HQ 611
Tien Moi	HQ 601		HQ 614
Kim Qui	HQ 605		

Displacement 95 (standard) tons, 143 full load **Length** 110 ft (33 m) **Beam** 21 ft (6.3 m) **Draft** 9 ft (2.7 m) **Guns** one 40 mm AA, two 20 mm AA (one twin), two HG **Main engines** diesels, 1,900 bhp, two shafts **Speed** 16 knots **Complement** 30.

Coastal minesweepers ex-US 'Bluebird' class MSC type

These coastal minesweepers of the 'Bluebird' class of non-magnetic wooden construction were transferred to South Vietnam under the Mutual Defense Assistance Programme in 1959-60.

Ch'O Ng Du 'O' Ng II	(ex-MSC 282)	HQ 115
Bach Dong II	(ex-MSC 283)	HQ 116
Ham Tu II	(ex-MSC 281)	HQ 114

Displacement 320 (standard) tons, 370 full load **Length** 144 ft (44 m) **Beam** 28 ft (8.5 m) **Draft** 9 ft (2.7 m) **Guns** two .20 mm AA **Main engines** two diesels, 700 bhp, two shafts **Speed** 11 knots **Complement** 110 (7 officers and 103 enlisted men).

Landing ships

All these LSMs originated in the USA during World War 2 but were transferred to France for use in Indochina in 1954.

Displacement 743 tons (beaching), 1,095 full load **Length** 203.5 ft (62 m) **Beam** 34.5 ft (10.4 m) **Draft** 8.3 ft (2.5 m) **Guns** two 40 mm AA, four 20 mm AA **Main engines** diesels, 2,800 bhp, two shafts **Speed** 12 knots **Complement** 75 (5 officers and 70 enlisted men).

Hau Giang	(ex-LSM 276 – France)	HQ 406
Ham Giang	(ex-LSM 9012 – France)	
	(ex-LSM 110 – USA)	HQ 401
Hat Giang	(ex-LSM 9011 – France)	
	(ex-LSM 335 – USA)	HQ 400
Huong Giang	(ex-LSM 175 – USA)	HQ 404
Iam Giang	(ex-LSM 226 – France)	HQ 402
Ninh Giang	(ex-LSM 85 – USA)	
Ien Giang	(ex-LSM 713 – USA)	HQ 405

Landing ships (ex-LSSLs of French and US Navy)

Doan Ngoc Tang	(ex-LSSL 9 – USA)	HQ 228
Le Van Binh	(ex-LSSL 10 – USA)	HQ 227
Linh Kien	(ex-Arquebuse – France)	HQ 226
	(ex-LSSL 9022 – USA)	
Luo Phu Tho	(ex-LSSL – USA)	HQ 231
No Than	(ex-Framé – France)	HQ 225
Nguyen Duc Bong	(ex-LSSL 129 – USA)	HQ 231
Nguyen Ngoc Long	(ex-LSSL 96 – USA)	HQ 230

Displacement 227 (standard) tons, 383 full load **Length** 158 ft (48 m) **Beam** 23.7 ft ((7.2 m) **Draft** 5.7 ft (1.7 m) **Guns** one 3 in, four 40 mm, four 20 mm, four MG **Main engines** diesels, 1,600 bhp, two shafts **Speed** 14 knots **Complement** 60 (6 officers and 54 enlisted men).

Landing ships (ex-US LSILs transferred via French Navy to Indochina in 1956)

Long Dao	(ex-LSIL 9029 – France)	
	(ex-LSIL 698 – USA)	HQ 327
Loi Cong	(ex-LSIL 9034 – France)	
	(ex-LSIL 699 – USA)	HQ 330
Tam Set	(ex-LSIL 9033 – France)	
	(ex-LSIL 871 – USA)	HQ 331
Then Thien	(ex-LSIL 9035 – France)	
	(ex-LSIL 702 – USA)	HQ 328
Thien Kich	(ex-LSIL 9038 – France)	
	(ex-LSIL 872 – USA)	HQ 329

The Long Dao *(HQ 327) landing ship.*

Displacement 227 (standard) tons, 383 full load **Length** 158 ft (48 m) **Beam** 22.7 ft (7 m) **Draft** 5.3 ft (1.6 m) **Guns** one 3 in, one 40 mm, two 20 mm, four MG and four army mortars (two 3.1in, two 60 mm) **Main engines** diesel, 1,600 bhp, two shafts **Speed** 14.4 knots **Complement** 55 (6 officers and 49 enlisted men).

Landing craft (ex-US LCU type transferred from the *Division Navale d'Assaut*)

HQ 533	(ex-LCU 9076 – France)
	(ex-LCU 1479 – USA)
HQ 534	(ex-LCU 9089 – France)
	(ex-LCU 1480 – USA)
HQ 535	(ex-LCU 9086 – France)
	(ex-LCU 1221 – USA)
HQ 537	(ex-LCU 9887 – France)

Displacement 180 (light) tons, 360 full load **Length** 119 ft (36 m) **Beam** 34 ft (10.3 m) **Draft** 6 ft (1.8 m) **Guns** two 20 mm AA **Main engines** three diesels, 675 bhp, three shafts **Speed** 10 knots.

HQ 536	(ex-LCU 9074 – France)
	(ex-LCU 1466 – USA)
HQ 539	(ex-LCU – France)
	(ex-LCU 1502 – USA)

Displacement 160 (light) tons, 320 full load **Length** 119 ft (36 m) **Beam** 33 ft (10 m) **Draft** 5 ft (1.5 m) **Guns** two 20 mm AA **Main engines** three diesels, 675 bhp, three shafts **Speed** 10 knots.

A utility landing craft (HQ 533).

OTHER LANDING CRAFT

There were 32 landing craft of the LCM type, 10 light monitors, 53 LCVP and 46 FOM: 150 boats of these types were assigned to the River Force in June 1965. These numbers varied as transfers from the US Navy took place as local conditions required.

Motor launch minesweepers (ex-US MLMS type)

The MLMS were 50 ft (15 m) launches acquired from the US Navy in 1963. There were twelve in total.

MLMS 150	MLMS 156
MLMS 151	MLMS 157
MLMS 152	MLMS 158
MLMS 153	MLMS 159
MLMS 154	MLMS 160
MLMS 155	MLMS 161

Support ships (Amphibious logistic type)

Eighteen landing ships of various types, landing craft and auxiliaries were adapted for fleet support.

Other support ships

There were a mixed force of about 200 small armoured vessels (see under Minor Landing Craft). In addition were assigned River Patrol Boats (USN PBR Mk 1 and 2) and the 'Swift' type fast patrol craft. (Both the PBRs and 'Swifts' are referred to in detail on pages 76-83 and 20-22.)

Auxiliary gunboats (Junk type)

In June 1969, the coastal junk force, the organization of which is described on page 37, numbered about 500 vessels. By this time the sail-junk had been disposed of and the fleet motorized. The motor-junks were armed with .30 and .50 calibre machine guns and their diesel engines were equal to speeds of up to 15 knots.

Other auxiliary vessels

The South Vietnam Navy was equipped with supply vessels of the trawler type, taken into service; oilers (ex-US); harbour tugs (ex-US 'YTM' and 'YTL' types) and a water carrier (ex-US 'YW' type).

As the Americans wound down their war in spite of their success in defeating the North Vietnam Army (NVA) in the Tet Offensive of 1968, more and more ships and small craft were assigned to the South Vietnam Navy.

SOUTH VIETNAMESE NAVY AFTER 1973

In 1973, after American armed forces had been withdrawn, the strength of the South Vietnam Navy was as follows:

7 Frigates (US Coast Guard High Endurance Cutters — WHEC type).
2 Frigates (Radar Picket — DER type).
8 Escorts (including 5 minesweepers).
1 Patrol vessel (submarine chaser type).
2 Coastal Minesweepers.
25 Coastal Gunboats (US Coast Guard Cutters — WPB type).
25 Landing Ships (LST, LSM, LSSL and LSIL).
10 Oilers.
26 US Coast Guard Launchers.
850 Patrol, coastal and riverine craft.
165 Auxiliaries.

Ex-US Coast Guard high endurance cutters

Of these the most significant additions to the strength of the South Vietnam Navy were the coastal gunboats and frigates. The 311 ft (94.5 m) vessels were the largest combat ships to serve in the Vietnam Navy and the only ones to mount a 5-in gun battery. All anti-submarine weapons are believed to have been removed prior to transfer. Seven high endurance cutter WHECs were employed (essential data on these vessels is given on pages 23-24).

Tran Quang Khai	(ex *Berry Strait*, WHEC 382)	HQ 02
Tran Nhat Duat	(ex *Yakutat*, WHEC 380)	HQ 03
Tran Binh Trong	(ex *Castle Lock*, WHEC 383)	HQ 05
Tran Quoc Toan	(ex *Cooh Inlet*, WHEC 384)	HQ 06
Thain Ngu Lao	(ex *Absecon*, WHEC 374)	HQ 15
Ly Thoung Ke	(ex *Chincoteague*, WHEC 375)	HQ 16
Ngo Kuyen	(ex *McCulloch*, WHEC 386)	HQ 17

The two radar pcket (DER) type frigates were: *Tran Hung Dao* (ex-*Camp*, DER 251) HQ 01 and *Tran Khanh Du* (ex-*Forster*, DER 234) HQ 04 (essential data on these vessels is given on page 25).

Twenty-five ex-US Coast Guard 82 ft (25 m) cutters (WPB) were assigned as coastal gunboats.

Le Phuoc Dui	HQ 700	*Tran Lo*	HQ 714
Le Van Nga	HQ 701	*Buit Viet Thanh*	HQ 715
Huynh Van Cu	HQ 702	*Nguyen An*	HQ 716
Dao Thuc	HQ 704	*Nguyen Han*	HQ 717
Le Nguc Thanh	HQ 705	*Ngo Van Quyen*	HQ 718
Nguyen Ngoc Thach	HQ 706	*Van Dien*	HQ 719
Done Van Hoanh	HQ 707	*Ho Dang La*	HQ 720
Le Dinh Hung	HQ 708	*Dan Thoai*	HQ 721
Thuong Dien	HQ 709	*Huynh Bo*	HQ 722
Phen Ngoc Chau	HQ 710	*Nguyen Kim Hung*	HQ 723
Dao Van Dang	HQ 711	*Ho Day*	HQ 724
Le Dgoc An	HQ 712	*Trung Pa*	HQ 725
Huynh Van Ngan	HQ 713		

THE NORTH VIETNAM NAVY

In the war with France, the Viet Minh had shown no head for maritime war preferring to assault the French fortress areas in Tonkin Province and fight the marine commandos borne by the *dinassauts* by ambush and mortaring from the banks of the Red River and other major rivers of the northern province. Although the North Vietnam Navy has some claim to fame in the annals of naval history with the Gulf of Tonkin incident (1964) described on pages 12-13 when a handful of motor torpedo boats effectively started the Vietnam War, this tiny force made up of small Soviet and Chinese vessels had little or no influence on the conduct of the ensuing conflict. In 1969, the North Vietnam Navy comprised the following small fleet.

3 Patrol Vessels
15 Motor Torpedo Boats
28 Motor Gunboats

4 Minesweeping Boats
30 Patrol Craft
24 Landing Craft

Patrol Vessel (USSR 'SOI' type)

Four submarine chasers of the Soviet 'SOI' type were transferred to North Vietnam, two in 1960-61 and two in 1964-65, but one was sunk by US naval aircraft on 1 February 1966.

Displacement 215 (light) tons, 250 normal **Length** 147 ft (44.6 m) **Beam** 20 ft (6 m) **Draft** 10 ft (3.4 m) **Guns** four 25 mm (two twin mountings) **A/S weapons** four ahead-throwing rocket launchers, two DCT **Main engines** three diesels, 3,500 bhp **Speed** 28 knots **Complement** 30.

Motor torpedo boat (USSR 'P6' type)

These wooden hulled MTBs of the Soviet 'P6' class were built in China and transferred to North Vietnam between 1957 and 1964.

Displacement 50 (standard) tons **Length** 82 ft (25 m) **Beam** 16.8 ft (15 m) **Draft** 5.5 ft (1.6 m) **Guns** four 25 mm AA (two twin) **Tubes** two 2.1 in (single) **Mines** four **Speed** 40 knots.

Motor gunboat (Chinese 'Shanghai' type)

These motor gunboats were received from the People's Republic of China in May 1966. Four of this type were supplied.

Displacement 100 tons (full load) **Length** 83.5 ft (25 m) **Beam** 20 ft (6 m) **Draft** 6 ft (1.8 m) **Guns** four 37 mm (two twin), two 12.7 mm **A/S weapons** eight depth charges **Main engines** four diesels, 4,800 bhp **Speed** 40 knots **Complement** 17.

Motor gunboat (USSR 'Swatow' type)

The Soviet 'Swatow' type motor torpedo boats were built in China and 30 were transferred in 1958, 20 more in 1964. Due to losses in action only 24 of these MGs remained by 1969. Pennant numbers ran in the 600 series.

Displacement 67 tons (full load) **Length** 83.5 ft (25 m) **Beam** 20 ft (6 m) **Draft** 8 ft (2.4 m) **Guns** two 37 mm, two 20 mm **A/S weapons** eight depth charges **Main engines** four diesels, 4,800 bhp **Speed** 40 knots **Complement** 17.

Minesweeping boats (Patrol type)

Four vessels for minesweeping, patrol and general purpose duties were reported but no further details are known.

Patrol Craft (Motor launch type)

Thirty patrol craft of this type were incorporated into the North Vietnam Navy before May 1966 but no further details are known.

Landing craft ('General utility' type), (US 'LSM' type), (US 'LSSL' type)

An assortment of 24 landing craft served a variety of purposes in the North Vietnam fleet and naval establishment. There were also reported to be some LCIs, LSILs and LCTs. In 1974-75 the strength of the North Vietnam Navy remained approximately the same as in 1969.

BOMBARDMENT FROM THE SEA

Allied land units operating close to the shore in the lowland coastal provinces relied daily on support from the Seventh Fleet to augment the fire power of their own artillery and tanks, strike aircraft and heliborne machine guns and rockets. Naval guns could reach targets in one third of the land area of I Corps and in most of the coastal provinces of II and III Corps. In addition, shallow-draft vessels bombarded areas in the Mekong Delta. Relatively safe from the enemy, the gunfire support ships cruising in the South China Sea could bring fire to bear by day or night and often in the worst kind of weather conditions.

The activation of the World War 2 battleship USS *New Jersey* was announced on 1 August 1967. The *New Jersey* was deployed to Vietnam from early September 1968 to late March 1969, after which she returned to her home port of Long Beach, California, for maintenance and refresher training. For this short spell in Vietnam the *New Jersey* was supported by four 8 in gun cruisers and four rocket ships for shore bombardment.

Throughout the Vietnam War, the warships of the Seventh Fleet's Cruiser-Destroyer Group acted as gunfire support vessels. Because the waters are deep along the coast of the northern and central provinces of Vietnam, the ships could move inshore to bombard their targets. The subordinate Naval Gunfire Support Unit, in coordination with Military Assistance Command, Vietnam (MACV), directed operations along the coast. Ships were assigned to the group from the fleet's cruiser-destroyer command and from the Royal Australian Navy, but were also temporarily attached from carrier escort units, the 'Sea Dragon' force steaming off North Vietnam, and from the amphibious force. In addition, the US Navy and US Coast Guard combat craft conducting inshore coastal and river patrols often provided gunfire support for allied operations.

Typically, one cruiser, four destroyers, one inshore ship (IFS), and two medium landing ships comprised the Task Force Unit. However, the number varied and totalled as many as two cruisers, eighteen destroyers, and two rocket ships during the period of heavy combat after Tet in 1968.

The ships and the weapons they carried were diverse. Heavy cruisers, such as the *Saint Paul* were armed with 8 in/.55 calibre and 5 in/.38 calibre guns, the former able to fire 26,000 yards (23,712 m). Light guided missile cruisers *Topeka* and *Oklahoma City* carried 6 in/.47 calibre guns with a range up to 22,000 yards (20,064 m), and shorter range 5 in/.38 calibre guns. While many of the fleet's destroyers carried the 5 in/.38 calibre gun, accurate at 15,000 yards (13,680 m), the more modern ships were armed with 5 in/.54 calibre weapons capable of hitting a target at 22,000 yards (20,064 m). Both IFS and LSMR carried 5 in/.38 calibre guns and rocket launchers able to propel 380 5 in rockets a minute up to 10,000 yards (9,140 m). These latter, shallow draft vessels were especially useful off the Mekong Delta shore.

Naval shore bombardment operations generally took two forms: unspotted fire on preselected areas where the enemy was thought likely to be found and fire directed on specific enemy troop formations, fortifications and supply facilities by aerial or ground observers. The airborne spotters were US Army or US Air Force forward air controllers flying O-1E Birddog aircraft, while the spotters on the ground were US naval liaison officers serving with detachments of the Fleet Marine Forces 1st Air and Gunfire Liaison Company. The observers, although actually controlling the naval artillery support, at the same time assessed the requirements of the main unit commanders, thus integrating the naval guns with the land battle. Softening up strong fortifications and entrenchments were also vital tasks of the naval surface ships.

During the first year of direct American combat involvement in Vietnam (1965), 72 Seventh Fleet ships fired close on 19,000 large calibre rounds, which destroyed or damaged 4,000 enemy structures, 66 small craft and inflicted 753 communist casualties. The cruisers and destroyers did not always operate as a task force. Ranging individually, destroyers hit targets such as Viet Cong supply caches deposited to support the communist seaborne infiltration effort. Cruisers and destroyers also took part in amphibious operations (see pages 57-72). On one occasion, in October 1965, the destroyer *Ozbourn* (DD 846) sailed right into the Rung Sat Special Zone to provide direct fire against a Viet Cong force attacking in strength.

From mid-1966 on, the majority of the gunfire support ships were concentrated off I Corps where the tempo of combat was heaviest and the geography most favourable for inshore bombardment. In one such action on 13 September, the destroyer *Stormes* (DD 780) killed over 200 enemy troops in three hours of firing. By November almost 40,000 rounds were expended each month by the surface group off South Vietnam. Throughout 1966 the force killed 3,000 enemy troops and damaged or destroyed 35,000 structures.

The involvement of the cruiser-destroyer-rocket ship group in coastal bombardment and amphibious landings saw an increase in 1967. The Naval Gunfire Support Unit was assisted by the arrival in Vietnamese waters of the Australian guided missile cruiser HMAS *Hobart* (D 39). This sea force fired 500,000 rounds, in 1967, approximately twice as many as they had the previous year, with the great majority of them falling on I Corps targets in the northern half of the DMZ and Southern North Vietnam.

The enemy's Tet offensive in the first half of 1968 during which the North Vietnam regulars, assisted by the Viet Cong militia, attacked over 100 cities and towns in South Vietnam, engaged the Naval Gunfire Support Unit in its heaviest combat actions of the war. The Task Force concentrated as many as 22 ships at one time on the gun line. These ships maintained high rates of fire during this crisis period, with the heavy cruisers firing an average of 800 rounds each day.

In February 1968, heavy guided missile cruiser *Canberra* (CAG 2), light guided missile cruiser *Providence,* and seven other surface ships poured fire into enemy targets near Hue, including the fortified Citadel, and played an important role in the allied recapture of the Old Imperial City, the ancient capital of Vietnam.

The following month, *Newport News* (CA 148) reduced the flow of amunition to enemy units when she destroyed an NVA logistic complex north of the Cua Viet River. In another instance, in May *Henry B. Wilson* (DDG 7) bombarded a North Vietnamese battalion, killing 82 of the unit's troops. In similar actions during the first eight months of 1968, the Naval Gunfire Support Unit inflicted over 300 casualties on the reeling communist forces.

USS NEW JERSEY ('IOWA' CLASS BATTLESHIP)

The US 'Iowa' class — the *Iowa, New Jersey, Missouri* and *Wisconsin* — were the largest battleships ever built except for the Japanese *Yamato* and *Mushashi* (64,174 tons, 883 ft (269 m) overall, with nine 18 in guns). All four of the 'Iowas' were in action in the Pacific in World War 2, primarily screening fast carriers and bombarding amphibious invasion objectives. Three were mothballed after the war, with the *Missouri* being retained in service as a training ship. All four ships were again in service during the Korean War (1950-53) as shore bombardment ships, all were mothballed again between 1954-58.

The return of a full-scale listing for the 'Iowa' class dreadnoughts followed the decision in mid-1967 to reactivate the *New Jersey* to 'provide an extended range and increased destructive power to the . . . Seventh Fleet bombardment group'. The US Navy had retained the four 45,000 ton 'Iowa' class ships long after other navies had scrapped or disarmed their battleships. Several proposals had been put forward to convert the 'Iowas' to underway replenishment ships, combination command-bombardment-assault ships, etc, but they had retained their existing configuration in the reserve (mothball) fleet.

The *New Jersey* commenced reactivation on 1 August 1967 at a cost of approximately $21,000,000 and was recommissioned on 6 April 1968. The *Iowa* and *Wisconsin* remained in reserve at the Philadelphia Naval Shipyard where the *New Jersey* had been berthed and reactivated. The mothballed *Missouri* remained at the

Above and top *The* New Jersey *bombards coastal targets in Vietnam, March 1969.*

Puget Sound Naval Shipyard, Bremerton, Washington. The *New Jersey* deployed to the Seventh Fleet in early September 1968 and brought its 16 in guns into devastating use in the gunline for a period of six months. Returning to Long Beach, California in the spring of 1969, a second deployment to the combat zone in the autumn of 1969 'contingent upon the status of operations at that time', did not materialize.

Displacement 45,000 (standard) tons, 59,000 full load **Length** 887.6 ft (270 m) **Beam** 108.2 ft (33 m) **Draft** 38 ft (11.5 m) **Guns** nine 16 in/.50 calibre, twenty 5 in/.38 calibre dual purpose **Main engines** four geared Westinghouse turbines, 212,000 shp, four shafts, eight Babcock & Wilcox boilers **Speed** 33 knots (but all four 'Iowas' have reached 35 knots) **Complement** 1,626 (70 officers and 1,556 enlisted men).

Armour The 'Iowa' class battleships are the most heavily armoured US warships ever constructed, being designed to survive ship-to-ship combat with enemy ships armed with 16 in guns. The main armour belt consists of Class A steel armour 12.1 in (31 cm) thick, tapering vertically to 1.62 in (4.1 cm). A lower armour belt aft of Turret No. 3 provided to protect the propeller shafts is 13.5 in (34 cm) thick. Second deck armour is 6 in (15 cm). The three level conning tower sides are 17.3 in (45 cm) with an armoured roof 7.25 in (.18 cm). (The conning tower levels are pilot house, navigation bridge and flag-signal bridge.)

Design The 'Iowas' carry the same armament as six previous battleships but have increased protection and larger engines, accounting for additional displacement and increased speed. Design includes clipper bow and long foredecks. All are fitted as fleet flagships with additional accommodation and bridge level for admiral and staff.

Gunnery The 16 in guns can fire projectiles weighing up to 2,700 lb (1,007 kg) (armour piercing) a maximum distance of 23 miles (37 km). Anti-aircraft armament varied from time to time (not listed in above data).

Modernization for Vietnam The *New Jersey* underwent an austere modernization in 1967-68, with the installation of modern communications equipment, electronic counter measure (ECM) equipment, a fog foam firefighting system in engine rooms, air conditioning in living spaces, a new target-designating system and a helicopter platform.

CRUISERS

The Newport News *(CA 148) a heavy cruiser of the 'Salem' class.*

'Salem' class

The 'Salem' class were the largest and most powerful 8 in gun cruisers ever built. Completed too late for World War 2 they were employed primarily as flag ships for the Sixth Fleet in the Mediterranean and the Second Fleet in the Atlantic. The *Salem* was decommissioned on 10 January 1959 and the *Des Moines* on 14 July 1961. The *Newport News,* which was extensively modified, served as a fire support ship in Vietnam Waters 1967-68.

Displacement 17,000 (standard) tons, 21,500 full load **Length** 716.5 ft (218 m) **Beam** 76.3 ft (23 m) **Draft** 26 ft (8 m) **Guns** nine 8 in/.55 calibre, twelve 5 in/.38 calibre dual purpose **Main engines** four geared turbines (General Electric), 120,000 shp, four shafts, four Babcock & Wilcox boilers **Speed** 33 knots **Complement** approximately 1,200.

'Albany' class

Fourteen ships of this class were completed; four being converted to guided missile cruisers — the *Boston, Canberra, Columbus* and *Chicago.* Only the *Saint Paul* remained in service as an all-gun cruiser in the Vietnam era.

Displacement 13,600 (standard) tons, 17,200 full load **Length** 673.5 ft (205 m) **Beam** 70.9 ft (21.5 m) **Draft** 26 ft (8 m) **Guns** nine 8 in/.55 calibre AA **Main engines** four geared turbines (General Electric), 120,000 shp, four shafts, four Babcock & Wilcox boilers **Speed** 33 knots **Complement** 1,146 (61 officers and 1,085 enlisted men).

The Saint Paul *(CA 73), a heavy cruiser of the 'Albany' class.*

INSHORE FIRE SUPPORT SHIPS

Carronade (IFS) Inshore Fire Support (LFR) 'Carronade' type

The *Carronade* was specifically designed to provide fire support for amphibious landings. Commissioned in the mid-1950s she was mothballed from 1960 until 1965 when she was recommissioned for duty off Vietnam.

Displacement 1,040 (standard) tons, 1,500 full load **Length** 245 ft (74.4 m) **Beam** 38.5 ft (11.7 m) **Draft** 10 ft (3 m) **Guns** one 5 in/.38 calibre dual-purpose, four 40 mm AA (twin) **Rockets** eight rapid fire launchers for 5 in rockets **Main engines** two diesels (Fairbanks-Morse), 3,100 shp, two shafts **Speed** 15 knots **Complement** 139 (8 officers and 131 enlisted men).

Clarion River (LFR 409) Inshore Fire Support Ship (LFR) former LSMR

St Francis River (LFR 525) Inshore Fire Support Ship (LFR) former LSMR

These ships were redesigned during construction in 1945 to provide fire support for amphibious landings. Originally 45 were built (LSMR 501-545). The original designation of Medium Landing Ship-Rocket (LSMR) was changed to Inshore Fire Support Ship (LFR) for the eleven surviving ships on 1 January 1969. The *Clarion River* (LFR 409), *St Francis River* (LFR 525) and *White River* (LFR 536) took part in coastal bombardment amphibious operations on the South Vietnam coast.

Displacement 994 (standard) tons, 1,084 full load **Length** (LFR 504) 203.5 ft (62 m) **Beam** 34.5 ft (10.5 m) **Draft** 10 ft (3 m) **Length** (LFR 525) 206.2 ft (62.7 m) **Beam** 34.5 ft (10.4 m) **Draft** 10 ft (3 m) **Guns** one 5 in/.38 calibre dual-purpose, four 40 mm AA (twin) **Rockets** eight twin launchers for 5 in rockets **Main engines** two diesel (General Motors), 2,800 shp, two shafts **Speed** 12.6 knots **Complement** 137 (7 officers and 130 enlisted men).

GUIDED MISSILE LIGHT CRUISERS (CONVERTED 'CLEVELAND' CLASS)

These ships were converted from light cruisers of the 'Cleveland' class. There were six ships, which were generally similar in design: *Galveston* (CLG 3 – ex CL 93), *Little Rock* (CLG 4 – ex CL

92), *Oklahoma City* (CLG 5 – ex CL 91), *Providence* (CLG 6 – ex CL 82), *Springfield* (CLG 7 – ex CL 66), *Topeka* CLG 8 – ex CL 67). The *Galveston* was armed with Talos missiles: the *Little Rock* and *Oklahoma City* with Talos and fitted as fleet flagships; the *Providence* and *Springfield* with Terrier and fitted as fleet flag ships, and the *Topeka* with Terrier. The flagships normally rotated as flagships of the Sixth Fleet in the Mediterranean and the Seventh Fleet in the Western Pacific. *Topeka* was decommissioned on 5 June 1969.

Displacement 10,670 (standard) tons, 14,600 full load **Length** 610 ft (185 m) **Beam** 66.3 ft (20 m) **Draft** 25 ft (7.6 m) **Missiles** (CLG 3), one twin Talos launcher, (CLG 6), one twin Terrier launcher **Guns** (CLG 3), six 6 in/.47 calibre, six 5 in/.38 calibre dual-purpose, (CLG 6) three 6 in/.38 calibre dual-purpose **Main engines** four geared turbines (General Electric), 100,000 shp, four shafts, four Babcock & Wilcox boilers **Speed** 31.6 knots **Complement** (CLG 3) 1,200, (CLG 6) 1,680.

DESTROYERS

Modernized 'Gearing' class (FRAM 1)

Displacement 2,425 (standard) tons, 3,480 to 3,520 full load **Length** 390.5 ft (119 m) **Beam** 40.9 ft (12.4 m) **Draft** 19 ft (5.7 m) **Guns** four 5 in/.38 calibre dual-purpose **ASW weapons** one ASROC eight-tube launcher, two triple torpedo launchers (Mk 32), facilities for DASH **Main engines** two geared turbines (General Electric), 60,000 shp, two shafts, four Babcock & Wilcox boilers **Speed** 34 knots **Complement** 274 (14 officers and 260 enlisted men).

The Orleck *(DD 886) a destroyer of the modernized 'Gearing' class.*

'Fletcher' class

Prichett was one of many destroyers acting in the fire support role in Vietnam. (For photograph see colour section.)

Displacement 2,100 (standard) tons, 3,050 full load, **Length** 376.5 ft (114.4 m) **Beam** 39.5 ft (12 m) **Draft** 18 ft (5.4 m) **Guns** four or five 5 in/.38 calibre dual-purpose, six 40 mm AA (twin) **ASW weapons** depth charges, two fixed hedgehogs, two triple torpedo launchers (Mk 32), torpedo tubes eight or ten 21 in quintuple **Main engines** two geared turbines, 60,000 shp, two shafts, four boilers **Speed** 35 knots **Complement** 249 (14 officers and 235 enlisted men).

AMPHIBIOUS LANDINGS IN SOUTH VIETNAM (TASK FORCE 76)

At 06.00 on 8 March 1965, the commander of the Seventh Fleet's Amphibious Task Force issued the traditional order to 'land the landing force'. Soon afterwards, *Vancouver* (LPD 2), *Mount McKinley* (AGC 7), *Henrico* (APA 45), and *Union* (AKA 106) began disembarking marines for the movement ashore. When it crossed the beach between 09.02 and 09.18, the 3rd Battalion, 9th Marines became the first battalion size American ground combat unit deployed to South Vietnam in the Southeast Asian conflict.

The landing at Danang that morning on friendly territory was hardly an assault from the sea of World War 2 proportions but those ships were a small token of the ability of the US Navy to deploy amphibious warfare ships in huge numbers. Amphibious assault or the capability to land troops and their equipment on a hostile, defended shoreline was not developed on any scale until World War 2 and by the time of the Vietnam War the size and speed of the vessels had changed, if not the basic concepts learned in the Pacific 'island hopping campaign', the Mediterranean with the Sicily landings and in the Italian campaign and the invasion of Northwest Europe.

The Tank Landing Ship (LST) was the key ship in naval amphibious operations. The Vietnam War forced the US Navy to activate all available mothballed LSTs and increase the construction of these ships. The LSTs were to be employed in Southeast Asia for amphibious assault operations, for cargo hauling, for unloading merchantmen when docking facilities were not available, and for replenishment and support of riverine and coastal forces.

In 1968-69, the US Navy revised its amphibious ship nomenclature to have all designations in this category begin with the letter 'L'. The ships affected were Amphibious Command Ship (now LCC *vice* AGC); Inshore Fire Support Ship (LFR *vice* IFS); Amphibious Fire Support Ship (IFS *vice* LSMR); Amphibious Cargo Ship (LKA *vice* AKA); Amphibious Transport (LPA *vice* APA); Amphibious Transport (small), (LPR *vice* APD) and Amphibious Transport Submarine (LPSS *vice* APSS).

The Seventh Fleet provided direct support to the land campaign in South Vietnam with its Amphibious Ready Group/Special Landing Force offensive team. The ARG/SLF was a powerful, versatile, and highly mobile formation capable of striking the enemy along the length of the South Vietnamese littoral and far inland.

During the Vietnam War, the ARG usually consisted of three or four ships, including 'an amphibious' assault ship (LPH), a dock landing ship (LSD), an attack transport (APA) or a landing platform dock (LPD) and a tank landing ship (LST). The force was often augmented with other amphibious vessels as well. The 2,000 Marine SLF was composed of a medium helicopter squadron equipped with 24 UH-34s and embarked in the LPH. A battalion landing team, reinforced with artillery, armour, engineer, and other support units, made up the ground combat element.

These men and their equipment were divided among the ships enabling landings on shore, by helicopter, by the force's 41 organic tracked landing vehicles (LVT), or by both methods. The fleet provided additional assistance for amphibious operations, including carrier air cover, naval gunfire support, logistic supply by Task Force 73, medical support by hospital ships *Sanctuary* (AH 17) and *Repose* positioned close offshore, and support on the beach by underwater demolition team, SEAL, beachmaster, and special communications beach jumper units. Naval personnel also served in Marine units as medical corpsmen, chaplains, and spotters, the latter in First Air and Naval Gunfire Liaison Company detachments.

The Seventh Fleet's Commander Amphibious Task Force (Commander Task Force 76) exercised operational control of the ARG (Task Group 76.5) and the SLF (Task Group 79.5) at sea. With the deployment of another ARG/SLF, assigned the designations 76.4 and 79.4 respectively, to the South China Sea in April 1967, the amphibious flotilla was divided into ARG/SLF ALPHA and ARG/SLF BRAVO.

OPERATION 'STARLITE'

In August 1965, the US command took advantage of good intelligence to launch an action, named Operation 'Starlite', that was perhaps the greatest amphibious success of the war. Discovering that the 1st Viet Cong Regiment planned to attack the Marine enclave at Chu Lai from a coastal village 12 miles to the south, COMUSMACV directed the III Marine Amphibious Force, the chief marine command in South Vietnam, to anticipate the assault and destroy the 1,500-men enemy unit.

Between 18 and 25 August, cruiser *Galveston* (CLG 3) and destroyers *Orleck* (DD 886) and *Prichett* (DD 561) poured accurate naval gunfire on the enemy concentration as Seventh Fleet amphibious ships *Bayfield* (APA 33), *Cabildo* (LSD 16), *Vernon County* (LST 1161) and *Talladega* (APA 208), and other vessels landed Marine units on the beach. Other elements were ferried inland by helicopter from *Iwo Jima* (LPH 2) and Chu Lai. By the end of the week-long battle, the 1st Viet Cong Regiment had been pushed up to the sea by three Marine and two South Vietnamese battalions and pounded by air and naval gunfire. At the cost of 45 Marines killed and 203 wounded, the allied force inflicted 623 casualties on the enemy unit, putting it out of action for some time.

OPERATION 'DAGGER THRUST'

By the end of September 1965, the US leaders were prepared to initiate an amphibious campaign against communist forces along the entire South Vietnamese coast. COMUSMACV and fleet commanders planned a series of raids, designated 'Dagger Thrust' by the ARG/SLF in support of 'Market Time' anti-infiltration effort against the Viet Cong bases, supply points and small units. The first three raids were carried out between 25 September and 1 October in succession as the group struck at target areas near Vung Mu, Ben Goi, and Tam Quan in II Corps but without finding any sign of the enemy. On 30 November the Navy Marine team struck at a suspected Viet Cong infiltration base on Cafe Ke Ga southwest of Phan Thiet and then at Phu Thu in northern II Corps on 5 and 6 December, again without great success. The programme was hampered by dated intelligence, some enemy foreknowledge of US intentions, and prolonged preparations.

The point of amphibious operations was to strike the Viet Cong where they were concentrated as a main force unit but beginning in October 1966, the growing menace from the North Vietnamese Army (NVA) units moving south through the DMZ drew the ARG/SLF to the northernmost reaches of South Vietnam. Before the end of the year Commander Seventh Fleet temporarily established an additional amphibious task force group, positioned just offshore for quick reaction. While 'Deckhouse V' was undertaken during the early part of 1967 in the Mekong Delta, each of the year's other 24 amphibious operations was conducted in I Corps. Furthermost ARG/SLF combat actions were in support of action against the fierce NVA thrusts at Dong Ha, Con Thien, and Quang Tri City and in the DMZ itself.

The amphibious force, permanently augmented by another ARG/SLF after April 1967, was often used to extend the allied flank at sea, block communist movements, land troops in the enemy's rear, or reinforce front line units. Troops landed by helicopter or amphibious craft and cruisers and destroyers provided ready, mobile, and powerful assistance. Noteworthy actions included landings in the southern half of the DMZ in May and operations in August and September to prevent the communists from disrupting South Vietnamese national elections.

The ARG/SLF accounted for over 3,000 enemy killed during 1967 but more importantly the force's support enabled other allied units to inflict even greater damage on the North Vietnamese Army.

The nature of operations remained the same during January 1968, when ARG/SLF Marines were lifted ashore by helicopter for four operations in I Corps. However, the enemy's massive Tet Offensive soon led to the long-term commitment ashore of the fleet's Marine forces and suspension of scheduled landings. During the next four months, the ships of the ARG served as havens afloat for the Navy's riverine combat and logistic craft deployed to the area and as supply transports. This sea-based support was crucial to the eventual allied success in the region. From June to the end of the year, ARG/SLF ALPHA or ARG/SLF BRAVO conducted nine operations that complemented the ground campaign in northern South Vietnam. The naval contingent played an important part in the general allied counter-offensive against communist forces in I Corps.

AMPHIBIOUS FORCE FLAGSHIPS/CARGO SHIPS

The Blue Ridge *'Mount McKinley' Class, amphibious command ship after overhaul at the Long Beach Naval Shipyard in 1976. Water is seen flooding Dry Dock No 1.*

Tulare *(LKA 112) of the 'Tulare' class of amphibious cargo ships.*

'Mount McKinley' class

Originally referred to as Auxiliary Combined Operations and Communications Headquarters Ships but designated Amphibious Force Flagships (AGC), five surviving ships of the 'Mount McKinley' class were redesignated Amphibious Command Ships (LCC) on 1 January 1969.

Displacement 7,510 (light) tons, 12,560 full load **Length** 495.3 ft (151 m) **Beam** 63 ft (19 m) **Draft** 28.2 ft (8.5 m) **Guns** one 5 in/.38 calibre DP, four 40 mm AA (twin mounts) **Main engines** one turbine (General Electric), 6,000 shp, one shaft, two Babcock & Wilcox boilers **Speed** 16.4 knots **Complement** 472 (36 officers and 436 enlisted men).

'Tulare' class

Displacement 6,456 (light) tons, 14,160 full load **Length** 459.2 ft (139.6 m) **Beam** 63 ft (19 m) **Draft** 26.3 ft (8 m) **Guns** eight 40 mm AA twin **Main engines** geared turbines, 6,000 shp, one shaft, two boilers **Speed** 16.5 knots **Complement** 247.

HELICOPTER CARRIERS
'Iwo Jima' class

The *Iwo Jima* was the world's first ship designed and constructed specifically to operate helicopters. (These ships correspond to commando ships in the Royal Navy, except that US ships did not carry landing craft.) Each LPH could carry a Marine battalion landing team, its guns, vehicles and equipment, plus a reinforced squadron of transport helicopters and various support personnel.

The 'Iwo Jima' class resembled World War 2 era escort carriers in size but had massive bridge structures. The hull continued up to the flight deck providing enclosed bows and flight decks. Each ship had two-deck lifts, one to port opposite the bridge and one to

Iwo Jima *(LPH 2), the lead ship of the amphibious assault ships (LPH).*

starboard aft of the island. Full hangars were provided but no arresting wires or catapults were fitted. Two small elevators carried cargo from holds to the flight deck.

Displacement 17,000 (light) tons, 18,300 full load **Length** 592 ft (180 m) **Beam** 84 ft (25.5 m) **Draft** 26 ft (8 m) **Flight deck width** 105 ft (32 m) **Helicopters** 20-24 medium (CH-46), four heavy (CH-53), four observation (HU-1) **Guns** eight 3 in/.50 calibre AA **Main engines** one geared turbine, 23,000 shp, one shaft, two 655 psi combustion boilers **Speed** (sustained) 20 knots **Complement** 526 (46 officers and 480 enlisted men) **Embarked troops** 2,000 (100 officers and 1,900 enlisted men).

DOCK LANDING SHIPS

The Casa Grande *(LSD 13) name ship of the 'Casa Grande' class of dock landing ships.*

'Casa Grande' class LSDs

The 'Casa Grande' class LSDs could either hold three utility landing craft (LCU) or eighteen mechanized landing craft (LCM). All ships in the class were fitted with helicopter platforms.

Displacement 4,790 (standard) tons, 9,375 full load **Length** 475.4 ft (144.5 m) **Beam** 76.2 ft (23 m) **Draft** 18 ft (5.4 m) **Guns** eight or twelve 40 mm AA (two quad, two twin) **Main engines** geared turbines, 7,000 shp, two shafts, two boilers **Complement** 265 (15 officers and 250 men).

ATTACK TRANSPORT SHIPS
'Haskell' class (LPA)

The designation of the surviving 'Haskell' class attack transports was changed from APA to LPA on 1 January 1969. *Talledega* (LPA 208) was typical.

Displacement 6,720 (light) tons, 10,470 full load **Length** 436.5 ft (133 m) **Beam** 62 ft (19 m) **Draft** 24 ft (7.2 m) **Guns** twelve 40 mm AA (one quad, four twin) **Main engines** geared turbines, 8,500 shp, one shaft, two Babcock & Wilcox boilers **Complement** 536 **Embarked troops** 1,560.

AMPHIBIOUS TRANSPORT DOCKS

The amphibious transport dock was developed from the dock landing ship (LPD) concept but provided more versatility. The LPD replaced the Amphibious Transport (LPA) and, in part the Amphibious Cargo Ship. The LPD could carry a 'balanced load' of assault troops and their equipment and had a docking well for

Cleveland *(LPD 7), of the 'Austin' class of amphibious transport docks (LPD).*

landing craft, a helicopter deck, cargo holds and vehicle garages.

Resembling the dock landing ships (LSD), the LPDs had a fully enclosed docking well with the roof forming a permanent helicopter platform. The docking well was 168 ft (51 m) long and 50 ft (15.2 m) wide, less than half the length of wells in newer LSDs but the LPD design provided more space for vehicles, cargo and troops. Ramps allowed vehicles to be driven between helicopter decks, parking areas and docking well. Side ports provided roll on/roll off capability when docks were available. An overhead monorail in the docking well with six cranes facilitated loading the landing craft.

The dock wells of these ships could hold one LCU and three LCM-6s. Four LCM-6s or two LCPLs could be carried on the boat deck and lowered by crane.

Displacement 8,040 (light) tons, 13,900 full load **Length** 521.8 ft (159 m) **Beam** 84 ft (25 m) **Draft** 21 ft (6.3 m) **Guns** eight 3 in/.50 calibre AA **Helicopters** six UH-34 or CH-46 **Main engines** two steam turbines, 24,000 shp, two shafts, two boilers **Speed** 20 knots (sustained), 23 knots (maximum) **Complement** 490 (30 officers and 460 enlisted men) **Embarked troops** 930

TANK LANDING SHIPS

There were many types of tank loading ships (LST) and they were specially converted for a number of roles. The *Garrett County* had a distinguished record on amphibious operations in the Vietnam War.

Displacement 2,590 (light) tons, 5,800 full load **Length** 384 ft (117 m) **Beam** 55 ft (16.7 m) **Draft** 17 ft (5 m) **Guns** six 3 in/.50 calibre (twin) **Main engines** GM diesels, 6,000 bhp, two shafts, controllable pitch propellers **Speed** 15 knots **Complement** 116 **Embarked troops** 395.

LST 337 on operational patrol.

Above *A Navy Swift boat (PCF 31) searches a Vietnamese ship in the Rung Sat Special Zone.*

Below *USS* Prichett *(DD 561) a destroyer of the 'Fletcher' Class*

Bottom *South Vietnamese frogmen prepare to salvage a sunken boat in the Co Chein River in Vinh Binh Province.*

Right *The amphibious assault ship USS* Inchon *(LPH 12).*

Bottom right *An LLC-1 offloads weapons and ammunition from a trawler after an arms find off the Vietnam coast.*

Below *South Vietnamese troops fire an 81 mm mortar from a commandament riverine craft.*

Above *The amphibious assault ship USS* Iwo Jima *(LPH 2).*

Below *A US Navy SEAL team ready for a Vietnam mission.*

Top Garrett County *(LST 786).*
Above *LCU 1493 utility landing ship.*

LANDING CRAFT, UTILITY

There were several LCU series. The LCU 1610 series could carry three medium sized tanks, and its diesels produced a speed of 11 knots. There was a crew of twelve per craft. The LCU 1466 series, of similar proportions but with fourteen crew, was fitted with three diesels and made a speed of 10 knots. A number of series 1466 LCUs were transferred to South Vietnam on completion. The LCU 501 series possessed Grey Marine diesels, which produced 10 knots and had a complement of thirteen per craft.

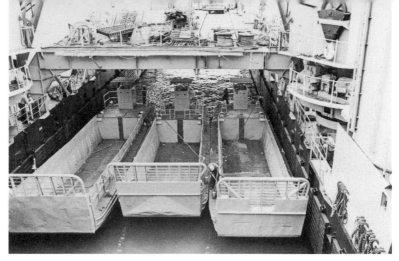

Three LCMs (mechanized landing craft) are floated out of the well deck of the dock landing ship USS Tortuga *(LSD).*

LANDING CRAFT, MECHANIZED

Constructed of welded steel, LCM 6 and LCM 8 types could carry a heavy tank. Two diesels in each type of craft were able to make speeds of up to 9 knots.

HELICOPTERS

The Sea Knight went into service with the US Marine Corps and US Navy as the CH-46A: for shore to ship to ship duties as the UH-46A uprated in 1966 to CH-46D and UH-46D.

The Western Repair Facility at Can Tho, IV Corps Tactical Zone, which covered the Mekong Delta area.

Above *Sea Knight helicopter (CH-46) Boeing-Vertol (USA).*

Below *This shot of the Sea Stallion gives some idea of the size of the USMC's workhorse.*

Power plant two GE T58-GE-10 shaft-turbine engines of 1256 shp each; **main rotor diameter** 50 ft (24.3 m); **length** 44 ft 10 in (13.6 m); **height** 16 ft 8.5 in (5.1 m); **maximum take-off weight** 28,000 lb (10.444 kg); **maximum speed** 144 knots; **hovering ceiling** 5,600 feet (170.2 m); **normal range** 200 miles (322 km); **capacity** 25 troops or 15 stretchers plus two attendants.

The Sea Stallion entered the US Marine Corps as the CH-53A in 1966, becoming operational in Vietnam in January 1967.

Power plant two GE T64-GE six shaft turbine engines of 2,850 shp each; **main rotor diameter** 72 ft 3 in (22 m); **length** 85 ft 3 in (26 m); **width folded** 15 feet 6 inches (4.71 m); **height** 24 ft 11 in (7.5 m); **maximum take-off weight** 42,000 lb (19,050 kg); **maximum speed** 170 knots; **cruising speed** 150 knots; **hovering ceiling** 4,800 ft (1459 m); **range** 222 miles (357 km); **capacity** 38 passengers, or 24 stretchers, or 8,000 lb (2984 kg) of internal or external loads.

THE WAR IN THE MEKONG DELTA

During 1965 and 1966 when the possibility of creating a US riverine force for operations in the Mekong Delta was being discussed, there were three basic considerations that weighed heavily in favour of the force: a tradition of past American success in riverine operations, going as far back as Union operations in the Mississippi basin during the Civil War; the success more recently achieved by the French in riverine operations during the Indochina War under conditions that appeared to have changed little during the years that had intervened; and most important, a situation in the Mekong Delta that seemed rife for exploitation by a riverine force. There were two main divisions of waterborne offensive to eliminate the Viet Cong guerrillas from the Delta: River Patrol Operation 'Game Warden' controlled by the US Navy's Task Force 116 and the Riverine Assault Force (Task Force 117), which was a combined Army and Navy effort.

By 1966 the communist forces had established both a political and military organization in the Mekong Delta. In mid-1966 the estimated strength of the Viet Cong in the IV Corps Tactical Zone (which corresponded roughly to the Delta) was 82,545 effectives (both men and women). Of these 19,270 were combat troops, 1,290 were support troops, 50,765 were local part-time guerillas, and 11,220 were working as poliitical agitators. At the time, no North Vietnam Army forces were reported in the IV Corps Tactical Zone. In the summer of 1966 the official intelligence estimates suggested that organized communist military forces in the IV Corps Tactical Zone consisted of three regimental headquarters, 28 battalions (eight of which were in the regiments), 69 separate companies, and 11 separate platoons — an estimate that agreed closely with that of US Military Assistance Command, Vietnam.

It was believed that Viet Cong logistics depended on support from the population, on captures from Republic of Vietnam units, and on weapons and ammunition furnished by the Democratic Republic of Vietnam and infiltrated by sea or by land from Cambodia. Areas fundamental to the Viet Cong logistical system, such as the Plain of Reeds, the U Minh Forest, and the Cam Zon Secret Zone west of My Tho served as sites for political, military, logistical, and training installations, and were supplemented by 'combat villages' on South Vietnamese territory, organized and controlled by the Viet Cong. Cambodia provided a rear service area for 10,000 or more main and local VC forces in Vietnamese provinces that offered free access to Cambodian territory.

The Viet Cong forces against whom the allies were arraigned in

1965 were as well armed as those elsewhere in Vietnam. The new family of 7.62 mm weapons manufactured by the Chinese communists were first captured in the Delta on 11 December 1964 by Republic of Vietnam armed forces. The capture included copies of the AK 47, the SKS carbine, the RPD light machine gun, and a quantity of M 43 intermediate 7.62 mm cartridges, all of Soviet design. During the same month, the Vietnam Army also captured the first RPG 2 anti-tank grenade launchers — a potent weapon when ambushing riverine craft.

Viet Cong communications equipment, while not abundant, appeared adequate and was able to interfere with and intrude on voice circuits of US and South Vietnam forces, blanking out transmissions and employing tactical deception.

Viet Cong methods of operation in the Delta were not substantially different from those employed by the enemy in other regions. In 1966 Viet Cong activities were mostly small unit operations — harassment, terrorism, and sabotage — with the Delta accounting for approximately one-third of all VC initiated incidents in South Vietnam but the enemy was also able to mount battalion-size attacks. Several times the Viet Cong demonstrated a willingness and an ability to slug it out with government forces.

In January 1963 at At Bac, a Viet Cong force engaged a superior Army of Vietnam force that was attempting to surround the VC by using heliborne assault in conjunction with conventional ground movement. Five helicopters were destroyed and nine damaged as the VC inflicted heavy casualties before withdrawing. In December 1964 two regiments of the Viet Cong 9th Division seized the Catholic village of Binh Gia. During the next four days the enemy ambushed and virtually destroyed the Vietnamese 33rd Ranger Battalion and 4th Marine Battalion and inflicted heavy casualties on armoured and mechanized relief forces. There were, however, also local land forces, who were opposed to the Viet Cong and who were of assistance to Task Forces 116 and 117 in their patrol and riverine assault force role.

In 1966 most of the Mekong Delta was included in the IV Corps Tactical Zone, although Gia Dinh Province, Long An Province, and the Rung Sat Special Zone in the north were part of III Corps Tactical Zone. The IV Tactical Zone was in turn subdivided into three division tactical areas. (The four corps zones incidentally were the invention of the South Vietnamese, and the Americans conveniently slotted their forces into them.) In the north the South Vietnamese 7th Division had its headquarters at My Tho; in the centre was the 9th Division with HQ at Sa Dec: in the south was the 29th Division with its HQ at Bac Lieu. In 1966, the South Vietnam Army's assigned strength in IV Corps Zone averaged 40,000 men. In addition to the three divisions, there were five Ranger Battalions and three armoured cavalry squadrons.

South Vietnam paramilitary forces included Regional Forces, Popular Forces, Civilian Irregular Defence Group (CIDG) troops (the Montagnard and Nung 'indigs' led by US Special Forces A-Teams) and the National Police. In 1966 Regional and Popular Forces manned outpost and watchtowers scattered throughout the delta. Poorly supported and highly vulnerable to Viet Cong attack, both these forces had high desertion rates. The CIDG troops and their Green Beret sponsors were employed generally (in the delta region) along the Cambodian border, as part of an effort to seal the frontier against Viet Cong and North Vietnamese movements of men, equipment and supplies. The National Police were organized as a paramilitary force after the manner of the French *gendarmerie,* and exercised similar functions. One of these roles in Vietnam was to capture the hated Viet Cong tax collectors, who aggressively imposed 'protection' money demands on the delta villagers.

With a few exceptions, the large towns served as either province or district capitals and in 1966 were largely under government control. All, however, were occasionally subject to terrorist incidents, mortar or rocket attacks, or assaults against outlying guard posts. The Viet Cong, furthermore, were choking off the flow of rice to market: in 1963 rice arriving at the market in Saigon reached a high of about four million metric tons; in 1966 amounts declined to about three million tons making the importation of rice necessary. The Viet Cong were getting the upper hand and a major initiative was called for to change the situation. Additional forces were one option but such forces would require bases, which were difficult to provide. It was against this background that the basic decisions for the creation of an American riverine force were made in late 1965 and early 1966.

RIVER PATROL FORCE (TASK FORCE 116) — OPERATION 'GAME WARDEN'

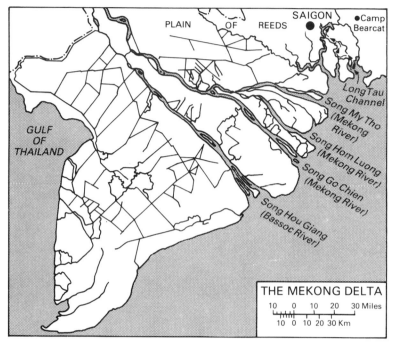

THE MEKONG DELTA

10   0   10   20   30 Miles
10   0   10 20 30 Km

The US Navy moved to ensure that allied forces would command the waterways when they established the River Patrol Force (Task Force 116) on 18 December 1965. From then until March 1966, the Navy procured river patrol boats (PBR) in the United States and prepared the crews at the Coronado and Marine Island, California. Although operationally controlled by Commander Task Force 116, the PBR boat force was placed under the Amphibious Force US Pacific Fleet command and given the designation River Patrol Squadron 5 on 15 March 1966. On 31 August 1968, the squadron consisted of 51, 52, 53, 54 and 55 headquartered at Can Tho/Binh Thuy, Sa Dec (later Vinh Long), My Tho, Nha Be, and Danang in I Corps respectively. The river division comprised two ten-boat sections which operated from combat bases along the major rivers or from ships positioned in the rivers.

RIVER PATROL BOAT (PBR)

The PBR, the workhorse of the River Patrol Force, was manned by a crew of four sailors, equipped with surface radar and two radios, and armed with a twin-mount .50-calibre machine gun forward, a .30-calibre machine gun aft, and a rapid fire 40-mm grenade launcher. The initial version of the boat, the Mark I, performed well in river patrol operations but was plagued with continual fouling of its water-jet engines by weeds and other detritus. In addition, the fibreglass hull of the boats was often damaged when Vietnamese sampans came alongside for inspection. The new Mark IIs, first deployed to the Delta in December 1966, brought with them improved jet pumps which reduced fouling, increased speed from 25 to 29 knots and more durable aluminium hulls.

The PBR design was adapted by United Boat Builders, Bellingham, Washington from a commercial fibreglass-hull (plastic) boat, especially suited for shallow-water operations with trainable water jet nozzles in lieu of conventional propeller or rudders.

Mark I (PBR 1-160 series)

Displacement 7.5 tons **Length** 31 ft (9.4 m) **Beam** 10.9 ft (3.3 m) **Draft** 2.2 ft (.66 m) **Guns** three .50 calibre machine guns (twin mounted forward, single aft), one 40 mm grenade launcher **Main engines** two geared diesels (General Motors) of 440 hp, water jets **Speed** 25+ knots **Complement** 4 enlisted men.

A PBR patrols the Mekong River near Dau Tieng during Operation 'Big Muddy', 1969.

Above *Another river patrol boat (PBR) transits a Delta river crowded with small craft.*

Below *Crewmen aboard a PBR man their weapons for close combat.*

Bottom *Men of an Underwater Demolition Team load a PBR with equipment they will need for a scheduled operation.*

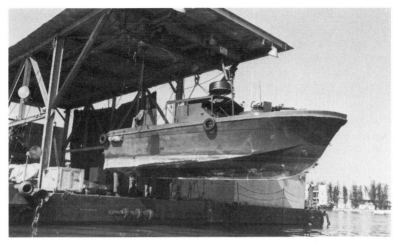

This scene at the Mobile Base One near Tan My, shows a PBR being hoisted for repairs.

Mark II (PBR 161-241) series

Displacement 8 tons **Length** 32 ft (9.7 m) **Beam** 11.5 ft (3.5 m) **Guns** three .50 calibre machine guns (twin mounted forward, single aft), one .40 mm grenade launcher **Main engines** two geared diesels (General Motors), water jets **Speed** 29 knots **Complement** 4 or 5 enlisted men.

Afloat bases

The afloat base concept introduced by the Americans was a significant advance over the fixed base system used by the

A PBR Mark II makes a high speed trial run on the Long Tau River, 1968.

French. However, a further refinement was introduced, in time, with the construction of non-self-propelled floating bases (LSDs). Five of these were eventually used by 'Game Warden' and proved successful. LSDs provided more space than LSTs and had the advantage of mobility over the land bases.

The afloat bases consisted of *Tortuga* (LSD 26), *Belle Grove* (LSD 25), *Cornstock* (LSD 19), *Floyd County* (LSD 762), and *Jennings County* (LST 846) during 1966. *Harnett County* (LST 821), *Garrett County* (LST 786) and *Hunterdon County* (LST 838) during 1967 and 1968. Each ship was reconfigured to provide floating base facilities for a PBR section and helicopter.

AIR SUPPORT

A key component of the 'Game Warden' operation was its air support element. Initially the Army deployed detachments of two UH-1B Iroquois helicopters and their crews to PBR bases and river based LSTs. Beginning in August 1966, however, air crews of the Navy's Helicopter Support Squadron 1 replaced the Army personnel. Then on 1 April 1967 the Navy activated Helicopter Attack (Light) Squadron (HAL) 3 at Vung Tau to assume the overall responsibility for providing Task Force 116 with aerial fire support, observation and medical evacuation. By September 1968, the 421-man 'Seawolves' Squadron controlled detachments of two helicopters each at Nha Be, Binh Thuy, Dong Tom, Rach Gia, Vinh Long, and on board three LSTs stationed in the large rivers of the Mekong Delta. The UH-1Bs, armed variously with 2.75 in machine guns, grenades and small arms were a powerful and mobile component to the 'Game Warden' surface units.

A US Navy UH-1 Iroquois (Huey) flies in close support of a Swift boat during Operation 'Slingshot' in 1969.

The UH-1B Iroquois was developed initially with 960 shp T53-L-5 turboshaft engines and first delivered in March 1961. Subsequent deliveries were fitted with 1,100 shp T53-L-11 turboshaft engines. Rotor diameter was 44 ft (13.3 m). Normal fuel capacity was 165 US gallons (624 litres) overload capacity 330 US gallons (1,249 litres). Normal capacity was two crew and seven troops; or three stretchers, two sitting casualties and a medical attendant; or 3,000 lb (1,364 kg) of cargo.

For armed support a rocket pack and electronically-controlled machine gun could be mounted on each side of the cabin. Other armament installations tested on the UH-1B included the General Electrics M-S nose-mounted 40 mm grenade launcher and XM-30 system.

The UH-1E entered service with the US Marine Corps in 1964. The UH-1E was the Marine Corps version of the Iroquois which was in widespread military service as a single crew, assault support helicopter.

NAVY COMMANDOS

The River Patrol Force commander led other naval forces as well, including the Navy's own commandos, the 'Sea-Air-Land' SEALS. In mid-1968, the 211-man SEAL Team 1 fielded twelve, fourteen—man platoons, each composed of two squads. Generally four or five of the platoons were deployed to South Vietnam, where one or two of them served with the special operations force in Danang and another three operated from Nha Be as Detachment 'Golf' in support of the Task Force 116 campaign in the Rung Sat Special Zone. Beginning in early 1967, the Atlantic Fleet's SEAL Team 2 provided another three platoons, two of which were

Crewmen ready their strike assault boats (STAB) for a night patrol on the Grand Canal.

Right *A SEAL team member finds the Delta deep and slimy as he makes his way from his boat to the shore.*

Left *A STAB boat makes a high speed patrol on a waterway near the Cambodian border.*

Below left *Navy crewmen aboard this patrol boat await the return of a SEAL team which has been inserted to raid a Viet Cong position. The scene is the Bassac River in the Mekong Delta.*

Bottom left *SEALS mounted in an assault boat practise taking up an ambush position.*

Below *A Navy SEAL team lines up aboard the tank landing ship USS* Jennings County *to demonstrate their skills to senior officers.*

stationed with the 'Game Warden' units at Can Tho. These units initiated SEAL operations in the central delta area. Although focused primarily on the areas to the south and west of Saigon, SEAL operations were also mounted in the I and II Corps Tactical Zones.

These elite naval units carried out day and night ambushes, hit and run raids, reconnaissance patrols, salvage dives, and special intelligence operations. Normally operating in six-man squads, the SEALS used landing craft, SEAL team assault boats (STAB), 26 ft (8 m) armoured trimarans, PBRs, sampans and helicopters for transportation to and from their target areas. The SEALS often descended from helicopters by abseiling before locating and destroying Viet Cong lairs.

Army Special Forces and a Navy Underwater Demolition Team discuss a beach clearing operation near Danang, I Corps Tactical Zone. This photograph was taken the day before the first two Marine battalions landed at Danang on 8 March 1965.

MINESWEEPERS OF TASK FORCE 116 (MSB)

Securing the rivers was nowhere more crucial than in the region near Saigon, the country's most important port. Viet Cong mining of the main shipping channel, the Long Tau River, which wound its way through the Rung Sat Special Zone south of the capital could have had a devastating effect on the war effort. Consequently, on 20 May 1966, the Navy established Mine Squadron II, Detachment 'ALPHA' (this became Mine Division 112 in May 1968) at Nha Be under Commander Task Force 116. From then until 1968, the minesweeping detachment operated a dozen minesweeping boats (MSB) reactivated in the United States and shipped to Southeast Asia. The 57 ft (17.3 m), fibreglass vessels were armed with a complement of machine guns, grenade launchers, and explosives. In addition to the main force at Nha Be, three-boat subordinate units were deployed at Danang and Cam Ranh Bay. In July 1967 Detachment 'Alpha's' strength was increased with the arrival at Nha Be of the first of six landing craft, mechanized (LCM(M)) specially configured to sweep mines.

RIVER PATROL

The 'Game Warden' mission was to deny the enemy use of the major waterways and it was a constant responsibility from the day

Task Force 116 was created (18 December 1965) until the end of the war. A section of ten PBRs operated with the responsibility for 30 miles (4.8 km) of waterway. Patrols were normally conducted by two-boat teams operating within radar range of one another for mutual support. With each boat section, one team patrolled during daylight hours and three teams patrolled at night. The fifth team remained at base to service the boats. Patrols normally extended over twelve hours.

The initial 'Game Warden' organization included a Delta River Patrol Group and a Rung Sat Special Zone Patrol Group. Of these two areas, Rung Sat was considered the most important because of its access to the port of Saigon. Four Saigon-based LCPLs with American crews were deployed to augment the South Vietnamese Navy's surveillance of Rung Sat in 1965. Shortly afterwards, a WPB and PCF were borrowed from 'Market Time' for use in Rung Sat, and in March 1966 four minesweepers (MSB) had been added. That same month, the 31 ft (9.4 m) PBR began arriving. The first of these modified Hatteras hull, fibreglass high-speed boats were sent to relieve the WPBs and PCFs in Rung Sat enabling the latter to return to their 'Market Time' assignments.

That the Americans attached considerable importance to Rung Sat is illustrated by their reaction to a Viet Cong attack on a freighter of Panamanian registry transiting the zone in February 1966 (a few days later, a Vietnamese fuel barge was also fired on). The Navy was asked by General William Westmoreland, Commanding General Military Assistance Command, Vietnam (MACV) to use its Amphibious Ready Group/Special Landing Force (ARG/SLF) to clear the area. On 14 March, a reinforced US Marine battalion landed in the Rung Sat for sustained operations that extended to 6 April. In the later stages of this operation, code named Operation 'Jackstay', two battalions of Vietnamese Marines joined in the sweep.

At the end of the first major action in Rung Sat, 69 enemy were dead or captured, key Viet Cong supply bases, training sites, and other logistical facilities were destroyed and enemy movement in the zone was restricted. PBR units, including one section based on *Tortuga,* minesweeping boats from Nha Be, SEALs, and helicopters consolidated many of these gains, but the enemy remained a potent and elusive threat.

In one month, August 1966, Viet Cong mines in the Long Tau heavily damaged SS *Baton Rouge Victory,* a Vietnamese Navy motor launch minesweeper, and MSB 54. In November, MSB 54 was again mined, and this time sunk. On the last day of the year, American forces discovered a Soviet-made contact mine in the shipping channel. Minesweeping operations by the US and Vietnamese units were intensified as a result, with the enemy continuing to harass them. In February 1967 communist recoilless rifle fire and mines heavily damaged MSB 49, destroyed MSB 45, and inflicted lesser damage on other 'Game Warden' vessels.

By the spring of 1967 the rapid build-up of allied forces in the Rung Sat area, the refinement of tactics and improvement of weapons systems began to reduce enemy effectiveness. During the year Vietnamese Regional Forces and the US Army 9th Infantry Division troops conducted aggressive actions ashore in co-ordination with helicopter, PBR and MSB units. The better equipped LCM(M)s augmented the minesweeping force at Dha Be. SEALs began sowing land mines throughout the enemy held areas, and both PBRs and MSBs now added 40 mm grenade launchers to their armaments.

During the period from mid-1967 to mid-1968, the Viet Cong continued to ambush shipping in the Long Tau with mines, 122 mm rockets, rocket-propelled grenades (RPG), recoilless rifles, machine guns, and small arms but the assaults were often cut short by the quick allied reaction forces. Thus, damage to ships and casualties were relatively light. Other attacks did not occur because PBR and SEAL patrols upset enemy plans or the MSBs and LCM(M)s swept up the mines. Consequently, the communists were unable to sever the vital lifeline to Saigon, even when their forces were fighting for survival during the Tet and post-Tet battles of 1968.

'Game Warden' operations in the Mekong Delta began properly on 8 May 1966 when PBR River Section S11 of River Division 51 began patrolling a stretch of the Bassac River from their base at Can Tho. Soon afterwards, other units initiated surveillance activities on the upper Mekong and on the My Tho, Ham Luong, and Co Chien arms caches to the south.

In random two-boat patrols, Task Force 116 sailors checked the cargo and identity papers of junks and sampans sailing the waterways, set up night ambushes at suspected enemy crossing points, supported the SEALs with gunfire and transportation and enforced curfew restrictions in their sector, usually no more than 35 nautical miles (56 km) from the base.

The following US Navy combat summary (after combat report), is typical of many and demonstrates the contribution of the PBR and crews in Vietnam:

'Viet Cong crossing thwarted — death of RM2 Freund At about 14.50 (local time) on 26 October (1966), PBRs 34 and 40, on normal patrol 42 miles downstream from Can Tho on the Bassac River, sighted three armed men in a sampan emerging from a stream on the southwest bank of the river, in an area known to be heavily infested with Viet Cong.

'The patrol gave chase and fired two warning shots at the enemy before opening fire with 70 rounds of .50 calibre which set fire to the sampan. The boat reached the beach and its occupants took cover in the tree line. One M-79 round was fired into the area.

'A Vietnamese National Policeman embarked in one of the PBRs directed a civilian sampan to attempt to recover the Viet Cong craft, but heavy fire broke out from the shore and the salvage efforts were abandoned. The patrol raked the brush along the river bank and quickly suppressed the fire coming from the area near the beached sampan.

'When fire from the immediate area ceased the enemy opened fire from farther downstream with a .30 calibre machine gun. The forward gunner in PBR 40, Radioman Second Class Terrance Jay Freund, 540 65 07, US Navy, was hit in the chest by the first burst and knocked to the deck. He struggled to his feet, told the patrol officer he was ''okay'' and resumed fire, then slumped again.

'Once again Petty Officer Freund returned to his post and continued to fire at the Viet Cong positions. He slumped to the deck for a third and final time. Petty Officer Freund had fired over 200 rounds of .50 calibre at the enemy between the time he was hit and the time he died.

At 16.30 a 'Game Warden' helo fire team arrived on scene and began to take the enemy under fire. At 16.40 PBRs 37 and 38 arrived in the area and were taken under fire by rockets and grenades from the beach.

'At 16.45 US Army helicopters joined the battle, and at 17.10 Vietnamese Navy RAG boats joined PBRs 37 and 38 in making firing runs on the beach for 40 minutes when they cleared the area for a US Air Force F-100 strike which was later cancelled.

'At 17.52 the Army helos, freshly rearmed, delivered more fire at the ambush positions. The Navy helos also returned to the area after rearming and carried on the attack.

'River Assault Group 25 of the Vietnamese Navy, supported by the PBRs entered a canal in the area and set up a blocking force behind the ambush. At 19.04, a RAG monitor entered the stream with two LCVPs and two FOMs and delivered 40 mm fire. Shortly after the monitor raked the area the Viet Cong broke contact.

'The engagement claimed one American life. There were four confirmed Viet Cong killed, one sampan burned and an estimated battalion size crossing thwarted by the combined efforts of US and Vietnamese Navy units, and Army and Navy aircraft.'

SEAL OPERATIONS

SEAL operations often involved quite small scale firefights as the following examples illustrate, but such skirmishes in which one or two Viet Cong were killed added up to harassment of the VC in the Delta on a significant scale.

On the morning of 2 March 1969, a squad of SEALs and one Vietnamese guide were inserted by sampan, 10 miles northeast of Vinh Long. The Vietnamese member of the squad was dressed as a Viet Cong and armed with an AK-47: the LDNN questioned an old woman as to the whereabouts of the enemy. The squad then patrolled to a nearby house and spotted two unarmed VC outside the house. As the SEALs approached the VC alerted those inside the building.

The house was taken under fire. Seven VC ran out of the front door and one went out through the back in an effort to escape. As a result seven VC were killed and one wounded. The house was surrounded and Viet Cong were sighted crouching in a bunker were urged to surrender. This failing the SEALs threw a hand grenade into the bunker killing all three of its occupants. Three sampans were destroyed and a complete B-40 rocket system as well as several personnel weapons were captured.

On 1 February 1970, a 'Game Warden' six-man SEAL patrol operating in the Rung Sat Special Zone set up a water-borne guardpost by LSSC about four miles southeast of the Nha Be Naval Base. The LSSC and its team took up its position at 19.15. At 22.30, the SEALs departed the position and sailing en route to Nha Be encountered one sampan near the bank of the Long Tau shipping channel. One Vietnamese suspect was detained and sent to Nha Be for questioning.

Although the US Navy was cautious in over-evaluating the success of 'Game Warden' 1966-67, the year 1967 saw heavy action for the 'Game Warden' force during which over 400,000 vessels were boarded and inspected for enemy personnel and contraband. In addition the River Patrol Force destroyed, damaged or captured over 1,400 enemy vessels. However, 39 officers and men of the United States Navy died in battle, another 366 were wounded and 9 were missing.

As with the other naval combat forces in South Vietnam, Task Force 116 was fully engaged during the Tet offensive of 1968. Because of their fire power and mobility, the PBRs were rushed to cities and towns that were under siege by the enemy. The river patrol boat units were key elements in the successful defence of My Tho, Ben Tre, Chau Doc, Tra Vinh, and Can Tho in the Delta. On the other hand, the Viet Cong overran the PBR base at Vinh Long, forcing the defenders to withdraw to *Garrett County*. Despite such temporary setbacks, by mid-year Task Force 116 had re-established control over the major Mekong Delta rivers and helped to cut short the Viet Cong attacks on Saigon.

The brown water sailors provided crucial support to allied forces fighting to contain the enemy surge in I Corps. Following temporary deployment of River Section 521 and *Hunterdon County* to the river areas south of Danang and to Cau Hai Bay near

Hué from September to October 1967, PBR units were permanently assigned to the northern reaches of South Vietnam.

On 24 February 1968, COMNAVFORV established Task Force 'Clearwater' under the operational control of the Commanding General, III Amphibious Force, to secure control of the Perfume River to Hué and the Cua Viet River south of the DMZ. Task Force headquarters were established on board Mobile Base II, a floating barge complex stationed initially at Tan My and later Cua Viet.

Because of the presence of heavily armed North Vietnamese Army units, the twenty-boat PBR task force was strengthened with monitors, armoured river craft, PACVs and landing craft minesweepers and authorized to call on helicopter, attack aircraft, artillery, naval gunfire and ground troop support. Convoys bristling with weaponry were required to maintain the line of communication with forward combat units. Minesweeping and patrolling were also important functions of the naval force. Task Force 'Clearwater' support during North Vietnam's Tet Offensive in 1968 was vital to the successful defence of Khe Sanh, the recapture of Hué, and the defeat of the enemy in the northern I Corps zone.

TAKING THE WAR INTO THE PLAIN OF REEDS

THE 'GREEN BERET NAVY'

The US Navy and the South Vietnamese Navy patrolled the navigable waterways but the US Army was assigned the task of handling waterborne operations on the flooded rice marshes and canals of the lower Mekong Delta region. The Plain of Reeds had been a haven for guerrilla fighters and fugitives for centuries and the Viet Cong put the swamp forest to good use. The Army force

Below *Members of a Vietnamese Mobile Strike Force check over their airboat before a mission in the IV Corps Tactical Zone.*

Bottom *An airboat of Detachment A-433, 5th US Special Forces Group, patrols canal near My An.*

Vietnamese National Police aboard an airboat check the identification papers of a young couple in the Mekong Delta.

assigned to the area were the elite United States Special Forces, the Green Berets.

The main task of the US Special Forces in the Vietnam War was to set up 'Civilian Irregular Defense Group (CIDG)' camps of which there were eventually over 300 in South Vietnam. The CIDG units were made up of local tribesmen (Montagnards with Nung mercenaries) led by a Green Beret A-Team. These teams of specialists housed the 'indigs' with their families in fortified villages and helped to grow their crops and with everyday welfare. In return the CIDG units patrolled the surrounding areas and in time provided Mobile Strike Forces which were equipped and ready to fight at an instant's notice anywhere in the Vietnam battlefront.

In the monsoon many CIDG camps became virtually floating bases. Until the combat airboats were introduced, the Green Beret Navy used a collection of sampans and small engine assault boats with outboard motors. The Navy also sent PBRs and other small riverine craft. Even with small conventional boats, however, Special Forces mobility was limited. Meadows of sea grass were dense enough to cause prop-fouling at low tide. Mangrove swamps blocked boat movement with 60 ft (18.2 m) trees and mazes of gnarled roots. Freshwater swamps, filled with towering cajaput trees, formed an unbroken jungle canopy. Small streams and canals hampered land movement. Rice-field dikes were generally low but tiny clusters of houses and Nypa palms, provided

Airboats are seen lined up on either side of a floating pontoon at Camp Boyd.

good opportunities for ambush. The deep ditches around vegetable gardens offered excellent trenches and escape routes. Grassy marshes could be set ablaze in the dry season, creating confusion and smokescreens. The primitive watercraft initially available at camp level afforded a flimsy method of transportation, easily subject to ambush.

The Aircat, combat airboat

The Special Forces believed that modified versions of the 'swamp buggy' then popular in the Florida Everglades, could add a flexible dimension to the increasingly dangerous operations in the Delta. The Hurricane Company's airboat was powered by a 180-hp Lycoming aircraft engine, was 17 ft (5.1 m) in length, weighed 1,150 lb (429 kg), and at first mounted a .30 calibre A-6 machine gun in the bow.

The Aircat was capable of a speed of 38 mph (61 km/h) while carrying a load of 300 lb (112 kg). They could skim over aquatic grasses and leap rice-paddy dikes, requiring only a thumb's depth of water under their fibreglass and Styrofoam hulls. Their versatility soon included patrolling, blocking escape avenues, reconnoitering, transporting reserves or supplies, and providing medical

A PACV returns to its base at Cat Lo in the Mekong Delta after a mission.

evacuation. Elaborate tactics were devised for racing over water and marsh in pairs, or in massed formation to raid enemy strongpoints. Even ambush seemed feasible if crews let the boats drift or if they silently paddled into position, opened fire and then turned on their engines and sped off in pursuit of the enemy.

The first two trained Special Forces airboat platoons arrived at

Viet Cong prisoners are taken on board a PACV.

SK-5 type PACV.

Moc Hoa under Detachment B-41's responsibility on 27 October 1966. Altogether 54 Aircats were allocated to nine Delta stations. Advanced and unit training were completed at Moc Hao and Cai Cai. The actual combat employment of airboats, however, had to be learned by the Green Berets on a trial and error basis.

Patrol air cushion vehicle (PACV) SK-5 type

Three giant US Navy air cushion craft and eighteen sailors were quartered at Moc Hoa during the last weeks of November 1966 and the first week of December. On 21 November the first of ten combined Navy PACV-Special Forces operations throughout Kien Tuong Province was launched. Each air cushion vehicle carried eight members of the Special Forces. The PACV craft ranged over the countryside, over both dry and flooded terrain, restricted only by tree lines, and high reeds — which caused them to stall.

One of the most successful PACV actions occurred on 22 November 1966, when A-414 engaged a full company of Viet Cong irregulars. Both PACV and airboat teams were called into the battle and soon routed the VC, who attempted to flee into Cambodia. This movement was quickly blocked by six helicopters that air landed a mobile strike force (CIDG) company to seal off any escape. After a fierce two-hour struggle, the entire VC company

94

PACV 'Monsters' on the patrol.

was annihilated, and only one CIDG soldier was wounded in exchange. Fifty sampans were destroyed, and an outboard motor lost in a previous battle was recovered.

RIVERINE ASSAULT FORCE (TASK FORCE 117)

TAKING THE WAR INTO THE MEKONG DELTA

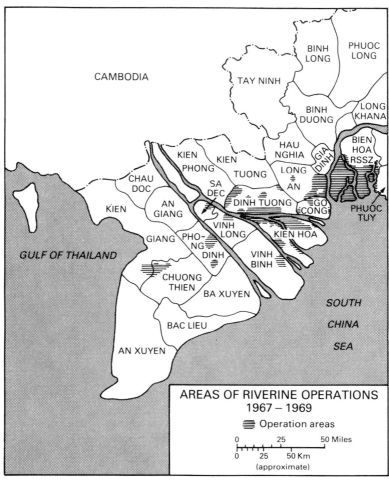

CAMBODIA

BINH LONG

PHUOC LONG

TAY NINH

BINH DUONG

LONG KHANA

HAU NGHIA

GIA DINH

BIEN HOA

RSSZ

KIEN PHONG

KIEN TUONG

LONG AN

CHAU DOC

SA DEC

KIEN

AN GIANG

DINH TUONG

GO CONG

PHUOC TUY

GIANG

PHO-NG

VINH LONG

KIEN HOA

GULF OF THAILAND

DINH

VINH BINH

CHUONG THIEN

BA XUYEN

SOUTH CHINA SEA

BAC LIEU

AN XUYEN

AREAS OF RIVERINE OPERATIONS
1967 – 1969

≋ Operation areas

0   25   50 Miles

0   25   50 Km

(approximate)

In July 1965 the United States Military Assistance Command, Vietnam (MACV) considered that the armed forces of Vietnam were capable of maintaining their position in the IV Corps, but not of reducing communist control over significant portions of the population and terrain in the Mekong Delta. While additional American and other 'Free World Military Assistance Forces' were planned for the other corps areas, none were planned in this region. In the opinion of the American staff planners, there could be no substantial progress in the IV Corps Tactical Zone unless US combat units were introduced.

As a preliminary step in studying the possibility of sending US forces into the Delta, the MACV staff despatched a team to survey the Delta for land suitable for basing ground troops. The surveyors, who looked at the My Tho, Vinh Long, Sa Dec and Can Tho areas concluded that all land suitable for large tactical units was either heavily populated or already occupied by Republic of Vietnam armed forces. If US units were based in the Delta, they would have to share already crowded areas or displace a portion of the population. Since neither of these courses was acceptable, the planning staff searched for other means of basing troops.

Eventually two land bases were decided upon: one for an infantry division headquarters and one brigade, and another for one brigade to be located in the northern part of the Delta, probably in Long An Province. A third brigade would be based on water. An LST could resupply the river force by travelling from Vung Tau across a stretch of the South China Sea into selected anchorage sites on the Mekong and Bassac Rivers. With the use of a mobile floating base, the mingling of US troops with the Vietnamese population could be reduced — a prime consideration in view of the reluctance of the Vietnamese to accept US ground forces within the Delta. MACV declared the idea of a floating base 'most imaginative'. These moves were to lead to the River Patrol Forces (Task Force 116) discussed earlier.

THE DINASSAUTS

If the Americans were inspired by the ironclad riverine vessels of the Civil War, French experience in the Indochina War 1946-54 was of more assistance to them in organizing riverine assault forces for operations in the Mekong Delta. In 1946 the French started out with craft that were available locally, native or left by the Japanese, who had occupied Vietnam in World War 2 modified with armour and armament. In addition the French received from the British LCAs (landing craft, assault), LCIs (landing craft, infantry) and LCTs (landing craft, tank).

The French army had created a number of river flotillas and in 1947 these were designated *divisions navales d'assauts* (naval assault divisions), abbreviated to *dinassauts*. Each flotilla, depending on its assignment and operational area had from twelve to eighteen craft, including LCVPs (landing craft, vehicle or personnel) to LSSLs (landing ships, support, large). LCMs (landing craft, mechanized) were operated by both army and navy while the army was also assigned amphibious vehicles of the Crab and Alligator type.

A French river assault flotilla generally deployed in column led by an open group of minesweepers (three two-boat sections and a reserve) with an LCM monitor out front acting as the guide. At a short interval behind would follow an LSSL or LSIL fire support ship in turn followed by two LCMs or LCTs and the transport element which might have been an LSM or an assortment of craft. When there was but one support ship, it took the lead and was the command ship. When there were two support ships, the command ship was in the rear, when there were three, the command ship was in the centre. The lead support ship might also be an LSSL, an armed LCT or a section of LCM monitors (two boats). Sometimes the transport craft were in two columns, lashed in pairs.

A flotilla ambushed and attacked by the Viet Minh would usually attempt to force passage using what the French called 'the ball of fire', or heaviest possible volume of immediate fire directed at enemy positions on shore.

In an assault the opening group (the guide ship and minesweepers) was followed over a distance of about 2,105 ft (750 m) by the shock group consisting of a command vessel, one or more fire support ships (to lay a pre-landing bombardment) and several landing craft carrying the assault troops. The remainder of the force trailed at a distance of 1,645 to 3,290 ft (1,000 to 1,500 m). Once a landing site was secured, the remainder of the landing force would beach and unload. During the landing and until the river craft were withdrawn, the force afloat provided fire support, protected the flanks of the landing site, and patrolled the vicinity to provide extra security. Some craft were used for logistic support, and the larger ships served temporarily as command posts for the ground unit commanders.

The tempo of French riverine operations increased steadily from 1946 until the end of the war in 1954. The *dinassauts* played a key role in the battles for the Red River Delta from the summer of 1951 through early 1952. Major battles were fought at Ninh Binh, 19 May-18 June 1951, 62 miles (100 km) south of Hanoi and on the Day River and at Hoa Binh, 14 November 1951-24 February 1952, 37 miles (62 km) west of Hanoi on the Black River. By the end of the war, French riverine forces were fully committed and were taking heavy casualties. After the war the French analyzed their experience with river warfare in Indochina. French *matériel,* they concluded, was generally adequate, although increased armament might have improved performance. French riverine forces proved highly vulnerable in base defence and were susceptible to water mines.

After the partition of Vietnam in 1954, South Vietnam naval forces attached to the 4th Naval Zone in the Delta included six river assault groups, evolved directly from the *dinassauts* and eleven coastal groups known collectively as the Junk Fleet. The assault groups were under the operational control of the IV Corps commander with the primary mission of supporting Vietnam riverine operations. Each group could lift a Vietnamese infantry battalion giving the IV Corps Zone the capability of a six-battalion lift. The river assault groups (RAG) in 1966 were used in their primary role only 10 per cent of the time. Vietnam Army divisional commanders apparently preferred helicopter operations to riverine transport and hence the river assault groups were employed only in support of small unit operations by Regional or Popular Forces under the control of provincial chiefs. Often they were used simply as escorts for commercial craft.

THE BIRTH OF THE BROWN WATER NAVY

The river force operating within the Mekong Delta was a joint Army-Navy organization and barracks ships were utilized to house part of the force. The barrack ships were supported by small landing craft, patrol boats and helicopters, such support enabling the river force to conduct operations within a defined radius of the floating base. In addition, the mobility of the small craft offered additional protection to the floating base.

Task Force 117, as the mobile riverine assault force was designated, consisted of a small fleet of ugly armoured vessels crewed by bluejackets and equipped to support assault troops of the US 9th Infantry Division. TF 117's combat craft numbered assault support patrol boats (ASPB), command and control boats (CCB), armoured troop carriers (ATC), monitors (MON) and various minesweepers (MSM-MSD-MSR). All naval personnel and the army battalion on active duty were embarked in the self-propelled barracks craft (APL). Maintenance and logistic support for the riverine craft were provided by ARLs and LSTs.

At Vallejo, California, the US Navy set up a training command (Naval inshore Operations Training Centre (NIOTIC) and preferred to teach the boat crews the basics of riverine warfare. Instruction was given in swimming, first aid, day and night navigation and those endless hours in the rivers and sloughs around Vallejo gave the bluejackets the start they needed. The sailors also received training in escape, survival and evasion at Warner Springs, California.

The US 9th Infantry Division was activated at Fort Riley, Kansas, on 1 February 1966 under the command of Major General George S. Eckhardt. This was the one infantry division to be organized specially in the United States for the fighting in Vietnam — the so called Z Division, scheduled for operations in the Mekong Delta. It was probably no coincidence that the division was designated the 9th US Infantry: General Westmoreland had seen extensive service with the 9th in World War 2, having commanded the 60th Infantry and served as chief of staff of the division during operations in both France and Germany.

The division in Vietnam was organized as a standard infantry division composed of nine infantry battalions of which one was (initially) mechanized. It had a cavalry squadron and the normal artillery and supporting units. The normal Army training programme was followed, but General Eckhardt instructed his brigade commanders to prepare their men for the physical conditions and the tactics of the enemy in Vietnam.

As 1966 progressed General Westmoreland became increasingly anxious to deploy more troops other than the riverine force (TF 116) already in place in the Mekong Delta. Overcoming objections from South Vietnamese commanders Westmoreland chose a Delta land base near My Tho. As the site did not have a name, the American General sought a significant name in keeping with the role as the first American base camp in the Mekong Delta.

The official MACV translator gave him several possible Vietnamese names for the base. The list included *Dong Tam,* a Vietnamese term literally meaning 'united hearts and minds'. General Westmoreland selected this name for three reasons: to signify the bond between American and Vietnamese people (with respect to the objective to be achieved in the Delta); it related to the objective of the introduction of US forces into the populous Delta and thirdly '*Dong Tam*' was a name which Americans would find easy to pronounce and remember.

An idea born in 1966 was to become an early 1967 reality. At the turn of the year the *Askari* (ARL 30), the *Henrico* (APB 45) and the *Whitfield County* (LST 1169) support ships were on their way to Southeast Asia with the first of the converted LCMs on board. In April the *Benewah* (APB 35), RIVERFLOTONE's huge ugly green flagship pushed over the horizon into Vung Tau harbour. The *Colleton* (APB 36) joined the growing force in Vietnam and in May the leading elements of the riverine assault moved to Dong Tam.

By this time, the 2nd Brigade, 9th Infantry Division was in country and in action in the Rung Sat Special Zone having completed training at Fort Riley at the end of November 1966. A brigade advance party had arrived in country in January 1967 two weeks ahead of the main body to give most of the tactical unit combat leaders battle experience before the rest of the force arrived at Vung Tau. On 7 February, elements of the 2nd Brigade commenced a one-week operation in the Nhon Trach District of Bien Hoa Province just north of the Rung Sat.

Mobile Riverine Force units rotated between the afloat base and Dong Tam, the main Delta base near My Tho. At this location the army's engineers and the navy's Seabees built a logistical complex especially for joint riverine operations. The base

Above *A member of a SEAL team uses caution as he watches for any movement in the thick wooded area along a stream.*

Below *A Patrol Air Cushion (PACV) displays its shark's teeth.*

Right *The USS* Benewah *(APB 35) moored in the Soi Rap River in the Rung Sat Special Zone with her assault ships alongside.*

Bottom right *A PBR at work alongside a Vietnamese sampan during a stop and search operation in the Perfume River, 1969.*

Below *River patrol boats (PBR) at work on patrol along the Mekong River*

Above *The armoured troop carrier (ATC) T-111-6 fires its high velocity water stream into an enemy bunker on the banks of the Van Co Don River.*

Below *An airboat prepares to enter the airboat docking facility at Camp Boyd, operated by Detachment A-404, 5th Special Forces Group.*

contained barracks, mess halls, repair shops, floating crane YD 220, a C-130 airstrip, small drydocks and waterfront facilities for the river craft. Further, the Army's 2nd Brigade Headquarters was located at Dong Tam.

Afloat bases

Altogether eight World War 2 barracks ships, all ex-LST type ships, were de-mothballed, but only the *Benewah* (APB 35), *Colleton* (APB 36), *Mercer* (APB 39), and the *Nueces* (APB 40) went into active service in the Vietnam War — the other APBs, the *Echols, Dorchester, Kingsman* and *Vandenburgh* were held in reserve in the USA. The *Benewah* and *Colleton* were officially recommissioned on 28 January 1967 for service in Vietnam. The *Mercer* and

The Benewah *and* Montrose *(APA 212) sit side by side in Vung Tau harbour shortly after their arrival in Vietnam.*

105

USS Colleton *(APB 36).*

Nueces were recommissioned in 1968. However, the *Colleton* was decommissioned in 1968 as the strength of Task Force 117 was reduced in line with the commencement of the wind-down of US forces in Vietnam after the Tet Offensive.

Displacement 2,189 (light) tons, 4,080 full load **Length** 328 ft (99.7 m) **Beam** 50 ft (15.2 m) **Draft** 11 ft (3.3 m) **Main engines** diesels (General Motors) 1,600 to 1,800 bhp, two shafts **Speed** (APB 35-40) 10 knots.

In view of the US and South Vietnam Air Forces' control of the skies over South Vietnam and the coastal naval zones, the 'mother' ships were virtually immune from air attack, as was the case with other allied naval vessels operating in the Mekong Delta, or in the South China Sea. The APBs were, however, attacked (unsuccessfully) on several occasions by enemy naval frogmen. The *Benewah* and *Colleton* displayed an armament of two 3 in guns, eight 40 mm guns (two quad mounts), ten .30 and eight .50 calibre machine guns.

The complement of each barracks ship was twelve officers and 186 enlisted men and the billeting capacity 900 men, which represented the 2nd Brigade battalion on active rosta and the naval crews who handled the riverine assault boats. For the troops and boat crews the barracks ships represented the 'Hiltons' of base facilities in an operational war zone. The living and most working places were air-conditioned. Messing facilities were sumptuous, particularly when compared with those in the field. Welfare facilities included rest rooms, a cinema, chapel, laundry, library and tailor shop. Evaporators produced up to 40,000 gallons (151,400 litres) of fresh water per day. A sixteen-bed hospital with X-ray room, a dental room and pharmacy were installed, and there was in addition a bacteriological laboratory for analytical research.

In addition to leading the naval combat flotilla, the Commander Task Force 117 also functioned as commander of River Support Squadron 7. This entailed responsibility for the Mobile Riverine Base from which one or two infantry battalions and one river assault squadron operated. The afloat base was made up of two self propelled barracks ships (APB); one LST (another LST steamed between the MRF and Vung Tau in a logistic support role); one specially configured landing craft (APL); a repair, berthing and messing barge (YRBM); two large harbour tugs (YTB); and a net laying ship (AN).

From 1967 to August 1968, in addition to the APBs already listed, the following vessels were at various times included in River Support Squadron 7.

'Terrebonne Parish' class (LST)

Vernon County (LST 1161), *Washtenshaw County* (LST 1166), *Whitfield County* (LST 1169), *Windham County* (LST 1170)

Displacement 2,590 (light) tons, 5,800 full load **Length** 384 ft (116.7 m) **Beam** 55 ft (16.7 m) **Draft** 17 ft (5.1 m) **Guns** six 3 in/.50 calibre (twin) **Main engines** four GM diesels, 6,000 bhp, two shafts, controllable pitch propellers **Speed** 15 knots **Complement** 116 **Embarked troops** 395.

'511 — 1152' Series LST

Caroline County (LST 525), *Kemper County* (LST 854), *Sedgwick County* (LST 1123).

Displacement 1,653 (standard) tons, 4,080 full load **Length** 328 ft (99.7 m) **Beam** 50 ft (15.2 m) **Draft** 14 ft (4.2 m) **Guns** eight 40 mm (twin) **Main engines** diesels (General Motors), 1,700 bhp, two shafts, **Speed** 11.6 knots **Complement** 119 **Embarked troops** 147.

Monitors

Converted from LCM-6s, monitors were heavily armoured with bar and plate armour and armed with a variety of weapons. These craft provided the fire support for the flotilla as well as security for the afloat bases. Some of the monitors were equipped with two Army M10-8 flame throwers in lieu of one 20 mm gun and howitzer or 81 mm mortar. These craft were popularly referred to as 'Zippo' monitors and the 'battleships' of the riverine fleet.

Above *At the end of the day's operations, river assault craft rest at the mobile riverine base.*

Below *A US Navy monitor, part of Assault Squadron 91.*

Above *A US Navy monitor M-91-2 is seen underway on the Mekong River.*

Below *A monitor uses its flamethrower (Zippo) to destroy a Viet Cong ambush position.*

Above *A boatswain's mate mans his twin .50 calibre machine gun mounted on board a monitor.*

Below *This converted LCM monitor displays a configuration primarily adapted for firepower support missions.*

Displacement 80 tons, 90 tons full load **Length** 60 ft (18.24 m) **Beam** 17.5 ft (5.3 m) **Draft** 4.5 ft (1.3 m) **Guns** one 105 mm or 81 mm mortar, two 20 mm, three .30 calibre MG, two 40 mm high velocity grenade launchers **Main engines** two diesels two shafts **Speed** 8 knots **Complement** 11.

Command and control boats

Similarly converted from LCM-6s and heavily armoured, the CCBs served as afloat command posts providing the command and communications facilities for the assault force and boat group commanders.

Displacement 80 tons full load **Length** 60 ft (18.2 m) **Beam** 17.6 ft (5.35 m) **Draft** 4.5 ft (1.3 m) **Guns** two 20 mm, two .30 calibre MG, two 40 mm high velocity grenade launchers **Main engines** two diesels, two shafts **Speed** 8 knots **Complement** 11.

Armoured troop carriers

The ATCs were clad with the same thick armour plating as the other converted LCMs and carried the assault infantry of the riverine flotillas, as well as small vehicles, field artillery and supplies. Some of the ATCs — unofficially called ATC(H)s — were fitted with light steel helicopter platforms to facilitate the evacuation

A command and control boat (CCR) constructed under Programme V.

Above *This ATC presents a sombre silhouette in half light on the Mekong Delta.*

Below *US infantrymen wade ashore from an ATC.*

Above *An ATC provides cover as an Army UH-1E Iroquois' helicopter* , *arrives to lift off a soldier wounded during a search for enemy munitions along the Vam Co Tay River.*

Below *ATC T-112-3 makes its way up the Mekong River.*

of wounded personnel. A winch fixed to the fantail for chain drag equipment was used to sweep for command detonated mines. A modified ATC also served as a refueller for the river fleet.

Displacement 66 tons full load **Length** 56 ft (17 m) **Beam** 17.5 ft (5.3 m) **Draft** 4.5 ft (1.3 m) **Guns** one or two 20 mm, two to six .30 calibre MG, two .50 calibre MG, one 40 mm high velocity grenade launcher, two 40 mm low velocity grenade launchers **Main engines** two diesels, two shafts **Speed** 8 knots **Complement** 7 **Troop capacity** 40 fully armed infantry.

Assault support patrol boats (ASPB)

Another converted LCM-6, the ASPB was specifically designed for riverine operations and served as an escort for other Navy river craft, also providing mine counter-measures during river operations. Hulls were steel-welded and the heavy scale of armament varied.

An ASPB moves alongside an ATC during a sweep for Viet Cong command detonated mines in the Mekong Delta.

Above *An ASPB and an ATC insert along a canal bank during a patrol.*

Below *An ASPB and PBRs move up the Rach Thom/Rach Mo canal system during an operation not far from Saigon.*

An ASPB patrols in the Rung Sat Special Zone.

The Sikorsky Aircraft Division of United Aircraft Corporation and the Stewart Seacraft Division of Teledyne Inc., developed the prototype advanced ASPBs for the Navy (designated Mark 2). These were later replaced by the 'Programme V' boats.

The Sikorsky craft, 50 ft (15.2 m) long with a beam of 17 ft (5.16 m) was powered by three gas turbines (United Aircraft of Canada) driving three water jets (Buehler Corporation). The speed of 40 knots demonstrated the potential movement of the ASPB in the close support role. The craft had a lightweight 105 mm howitzer gun and two 20 mm cannon mounted in a tank-like turret with a 360 degree field of fire. A smaller forward mount was remote controlled and initially contained two 7.62 mm machine guns and a 40 mm grenade launcher, but Sikorsky proposed replacing the machine guns with two 20 mm cannon. Also fitted for minesweeping, a radar tripod mast was placed aft. The Stewart Seacraft ASPB was similar but had a 81 mm mortar at first, in lieu of the 105 mm howitzer. Both craft were heavily armoured and designed with the main turret and engines on shock springs to reduce the effects of mine explosions.

The ASPB Programme V displayed, in addition to the howitzer or mortar, one or two 20 mm guns with .50 calibre MGs mounted in boats with only one 20 mm gun, two .30 calibre machine guns and

Crewmen on a severely damaged troop carrier try desperately to save their vessel from sinking while returning Viet Cong fire.

two 40 mm high velocity grenade launchers. The two .50 calibre machine guns were often placed in the forward turret, replacing a 20 mm single gun.

Displacement (ProgrammeV) 36.25 tons full load **Length** 50 ft (15.2 m) **Beam** 17 ft (5.16 m) **Draft** 4.5 ft (1.3 m) **Main engines** two diesels, two shafts **Speed** 15 knots **Complement** 6.

Patrol minesweepers (Modified ASPBs)

This modified ASPB design was fitted with bow mine deflectors and minesweeping gear to sweep moored and bottom mines in shallow water.

Displacement 36.25 tons full load **Length** 50 ft (15.2 m) **Beam** 17 ft (5.6 m) **Draft** 4.5 ft (1.3 m) **Guns** two .50 calibre MG **Main engines** two diesels, two shafts **Speed** 20 knots **Complement** 4 or 5.

River minesweeper (MSM) Programme V

These craft were converted from LCM-6 landing craft for

minesweeping. They were heavily armoured in the style of the assault riverine fleet. The 20 mm guns were mounted amidships in 'turrets' one to port and one to starboard. The MSMs could sweep moored and bottom mines in shallow waters.

Displacement 36.25 tons full load **Length** 60 ft (17 m) **Beam** 17 ft (5.6 m) **Draft** 4.5 ft (1.3 m) **Guns** two 20 mm, one .50 calibre MG, two 40 mm grenade launchers **Main engines** two diesels, two shafts **Speed** (when minesweeping) 8 knots, maximum 10 knots **Complement** 4 or 5.

IN ACTION WITH THE RIVERINE ASSAULT FORCE

As fully organized, the Mobile Riverine Force consisted of the army element, the 2nd Brigade of the 9th Infantry Division, augmented in mid-1968 by the 3rd Brigade, and the Navy element. Under COMUSMACV's overall direction, the Commanding General II Field Force, Vietnam, exercised operational control of the Army contingent, designated the Riverine Assault Force (Task Force 117). Commander Task Force 117, (also administratively titled Commander River Assault Flotilla 1) directed the operations of River Assault Squadrons (also assigned task group numerical designations) 9 and 11. After June 1968 squadrons 13 and 15 joined the force. That same month, the task force was reorganized into Mobile Riverine Group Alpha containing squadrons 9 and 11, and Mobile Riverine Group Bravo, controlling squadrons 13 and 15.

The brigade commander or a higher echelon Army commander usually selected the enemy target and area of operations. The two commanders then agreed upon the general task organization, the tentative duration and timing of the operation and the location of the mobile riverine base to support the operation. The planning often included great detail in order to ensure that major issues were resolved early on, permitting the two staffs to plan effectively.

In mounting a riverine assault operation, there were a number of special factors to be taken into consideration. The planning staff, using the commander's guidance, began by outlining the scheme of manoeuvre in the objective area. From there the planners worked backwards, covering in turn the landing or assault, water movement, and loading phases. Special considerations included tides, water depth, water obstructions, bridge clearance, distance of the mobile riverine base from beaches, availability of waterway routes into the area of operations, suitability of river banks for landing sites, and mooring for barge-mounted artillery.

The operational order which embodied such information further included the fire support plan, naval support plan, signal nets, logistics, civil affairs and psychological operations information. The intelligence annex of the field order supplied details on terrain, weather and the enemy situation. Waterway intelligence was usually provided in an appendix that covered hydrography and the enemy threat to assault craft. A map of the waterways to be used was furnished showing tides, widths and depths of streams, obstacles of various types, bridges, shoals, mud banks and other navigation data.

The original Afloat Force plan did not provide effective artillery support for Mobile Riverine Force operations. The armoured troop carriers (ATC) were capable of lifting the 105 mm howitzers and their prime movers and it was expected that the artillery battalion, after being moved by water, would establish firing positions at a suitable place on the bank. Terrain and reconnaissance in the Mekong Delta, however, soon convinced the 2nd Brigade planners that the off-loading of the prime movers from an ATC would greatly restrict operations because of the varying tides and the steepness of the river banks.

Consequently the Commanding Officer, 3rd Battalion, 34th Artillery, Lieutenant Colonel Carroll S. Meek, began an experiment with barge mounted artillery. He placed a 105 mm howitzer on a barge, using cleats and segments of telephone poles against which the trails of the howitzer rested. Successful firing demonstrated the feasibility of the method. By the use of aiming stakes placed ashore, routine fire support could be provided from the barges anchored securely against the river bank.

Further firing experiments in the Mekong Delta proved the barge unsatisfactory in that the high bow of the pontoon was nearly perpendicular to the surface of the water, making it hard to manoeuvre and tow, especially against the current, tide or prevailing wind. The barge was redesigned so that it floated lower in the water and had a sloped bow. After further experiments with the design at Cam Ranh Bay, six artillery barges were fabricated to accommodate two 105 mm howitzers. Each barge was towed by an LCM-8 throughout the areas in which the navy assault craft supported army forces.

Typical company landing formation.

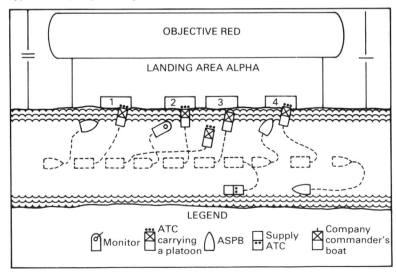

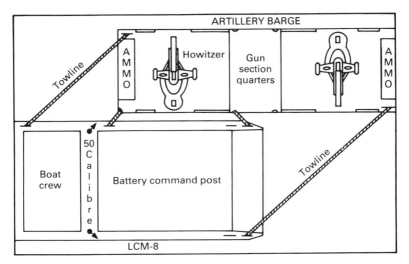

The artillery barge was a further US measure to overcome the difficulty of moving troops and firepower overland.

No two riverine assault operations were the same. Yet over the first and crucial year, a pattern developed. The day before a scheduled operation, crews loaded their boats with water, fuel, ammunition and C-rations. The boats were checked from top to bottom, anything fixed that might give trouble the following day.

That evening the boat captains assembled aboard the flagship (such as *Benewah*) for the briefing. Essential orders were distributed: movement plans, check points, signal schedules, codes and intelligence reports were noted. The order of loading and steaming was put out and the circle disassembled. Groping their way in the dark back to their boats the word was passed to the crews. Then the checklists were checked and rechecked, the night watch was set and the rest of the crew grabbed a couple of hours sleep.

Early in the morning, usually before dawn, the exact time being determined by the distance to the landing zone, the boats slipped their moorings alongside their barracks ship and formed up into a circle. The troop carriers returned to the APB to pick up a company of soldiers, who had also received their orders the previous evening. One reserve ATC stood by and ready to move in, in case one of the three ATCs was in trouble. Once the company was on board, the boats cast off and rejoined the circle. Then the monitors, command and control boats came alongside to pick up the command personnel.

On the signal to get underway, two minesweepers would head out into the new day and the circling boats pulled off into a long silent, fearsome column behind them. The troops aboard the ATCs lost little time in draping themselves over the steel decks, ammo boxes and each other to read or sleep their way to the point where the boats turned off the rivers to head down the smaller waterways. Here the sweeps were ordered to stream their gear: general quarters was signalled and the sailors took refuge in their flak jackets, steel posts and gun mounts.

The minesweepers leading the column were normally ASPBs which also provided fire support. Rifle companies were usually embarked in a River Assault Section consisting of one monitor and three ATCs. Boats within a section maintained 5 to 11 yards (5 to 10 m) intervals when under way; 164 to 328 yards (150 to 300 m) intervals were maintained between sections.

As the boats moved into small streams leading to their objective, a helicopter would be employed overhead for aerial reconnaissance. Sometimes the Air Force would also bomb the landing zones. Other times Army artillery pounded the area. Not infrequently a combination of the two was used. Arriving at the landing zones shortly after dawn boats would turn on signal in groups and run their bows up to the stream banks with the lead minesweeper and monitors moved in to cover their positions. The safety hooks came off and the bow ramps went down. Troops were always disembarked with their weapons poised for action. It may have been in mangrove swamps, rice paddies or palm thickets but the troops knew only too well that whatever the cover, the same, miserable Mekong mud would be under it.

After the landing some would back off and establish blocking patrols: others beached and watched and waited. Whilst the troops were ashore sampans were stopped and searched, men whose identification papers were not in order were detained for questioning by Vietnamese officials and war supplies confiscated. The riverine force could be called in to give fire support to suppress a Viet Cong position, re-supply the troops or move them to another location. Some boats were assigned special missions. A medical aid station, carrying doctors, medics, medical supplies and a built-in helo-pad, went upstream to pick up casualties. An ATC acted as a fuel bowser and another fitted with a landing-pad was ready to refuel helicopters. Marines assigned to these missions specialized in gathering information on water depths, currents and tides in the uncharted streams. An Explosive Ordnance Disposal (EOD) Team was also embarked on an ATC and ready to blow up anything that might impede progress or help the enemy.

After two or three days when the infantry had finished their sweep by night and day or when a battle was over if they had encountered the enemy in force, the boats closed in to pick them up. At the sight of the identifying smoke grenade, the boats lowered the ramps, and the wet, muddy, exhausted soldiers emerged from the bushes and clambered on board. The trip back to the MRB was usually a happier one than the inward journey. War stories grew in dimension as they were retold throughout the boats. Talk was about wives, girlfriends, and cars, as all troops concerned were happy to be alive and heading back to safety and the comfort of the mobile river base.

The next day or the day after, the boat crews would check out their boats, load them with C-rations, water, fuel and ammunition, the boat captains would be on their way again to the evening briefing . . . for the river squadrons, the MRB meant a hot shower and hot soup. It was like no other Navy outfit the sailors had seen before. The MRB was home, the ship's company family, it was a camp without liberty, a home that would probably never see the home port.

For the Army, the MRB was the greatest thing going for them in Vietnam. Even a 'no beer' policy was a fair exchange for a good 'rack' and air-conditioning. To the outside world the MRB was a focal point of a great new concept — an afloat riverine task force capable of penetrating the Mekong Delta. Each MRB vessel served a function essential to the force. No two ships served precisely the same purpose and without any one of them the force would have been severely crippled if not incapacitated.

The flagship *Benewah* (APB 35) carried the Army and Navy Commanders and their staffs, an RAD and an assortment of artillery and reconnaissance personnel. She carried as much communications equipment as a guided missile destroyer and received more visitors than a Yankee Station carrier, and the flight deck got almost as much traffic. Sister ship *Colleton* (APB 36) carried an RAS staff, one of the Army battalions, and an RAD. Her main job was the support of over 1,000 troops and sailors who made their home aboard it. APL-26, the green apple, was the only non self-propelled US ship in the assault task force. Designed for 500 people, she slept 700, over 125 of which shared the penthouse. Another noteworthy support ship was the 'Can do' repair shop *Askari* (APL 36), whose motto was 'adjustable'. *Askari* made a major contribution to keeping the ships and boats of the MRB in tip top condition and it was said that her crews would probably have made gold out of lead if asked to do it.

From its earliest operation in the Rung Sat Special Zone, action by the MRF ranged far and wide over the Mekong Delta. The first major battle occurred between 19 and 21 June 1967 when the Army-Navy team trapped three Viet Cong companies about 15 miles (24 km) south of Saigon and killed 255 communist troops. Another 59 of the enemy died in this area during July. Reacting to intelligence that two Viet Cong battalions were preparing to attack Dong Tam base, the Mobile Riverine Base ships weighed anchor;

steamed 61 miles (98 km) upriver to a new site; and joined with Vietnamese Marines, Vietnamese Army and US Army in attacking and scattering surprised units. The MRF recorded success of another sort in September when a landing and sweep manoeuvre in the eastern Rung Sat uncovered a cache of 105 rifles and machine guns, 165 grenades, 60 howitzer and mortar shells, and 56,000 rounds of small arms ammunition.

The MRF launched a series of operations against the Viet Cong over 1967-68 code named 'Coronado'. During Coronado V in September 1967, the Viet Cong who had been adjusting to MRF tactics struck back with an ambush along a two-mile (3.2 km) stretch of the Bai Lai River southeast of Saigon. At the end of the four-hour engagement half of the vessels in the convoy had been hit by enemy fire: three sailors were dead and 77 wounded. In October, however, the Vietnamese Army 7th Division, succeeded in trapping elements of the Viet Cong 263rd and 514th Main Force Battalions and inflicted 173 casualties on these units.

From October to the end of November 1967 the Mobile Riverine Force focused on reported troop concentrations north of the Mekong between Sa Dec and Dong Tam, but the enemy avoided significant contact. Then on 4 December, the Viet Cong tripped an ambush against River Assault Division 112 on the Ruong Canal northeast of Sa Dec. The river sailors turned the tables on the enemy when they fought through the ambush and landed troops on the enemy flank. Soon, other American and Vietnamese combat units surrounded and killed 266 Viet Cong and captured 321 small arms and 5,000 rounds of ammunition.

The actions of the MRF during the Tet offensive of 1968 were key to the allied military success in the Delta and earned the force the Presidential Unit Citation. Exploiting the inherent mobility and fire power of the riverine command during the first week of February 1968, the MRF battled through the streets of My Tho and helped recapture the overrun city, and then shifted to Vinh Long for several days of intense combat with three Viet Cong battalions. For the rest of the month the Army-Navy team fought around the Delta's chief city Can Tho. The force killed 644 enemy combatants in this patrol of continual crisis.

In July and August 1968 the Mobile Riverine Force ranged throughout the Delta with its now full complement of river craft, support ships and 9th Division troops. In the latter month, the MRF joined with other Army and Navy units and with the Vietnamese forces in a large-scale penetration of the U Minh Forest, long a Viet Cong stronghold. Although the enemy fiercely resisted this intrusion, inflicting heavy casualties, this allied military presence was maintained and heralded subsequent operations to deny the communist security in all areas of the Delta. Having demonstrated their worth during two years of combat, Mobile Riverine Force units would be in the vanguard of this campaign.

The following account based on after combat reports is taken from the Commander US Naval Forces Vietnam, *Monthly Historical Supplement,* April 1968, shortly after the commencement of the Tet Offensive.

'On the morning of 4 April the MRF launched a two battalion riverine and reconnaissance-in-force operation in Truc Giang and Giong Trom districts of Kien Hoa Province. The operation was initiated before dawn when RAD 8's 91 and 92 lifted the 4/47th and 3/47th Infantry into the Truc Giang operating area after Task Force SIXGUN had been established in its fire support base (FSPB) on the Cua Tieu River 7 miles east-southwest of My Tho. Shortly after dawn the mobile riverine base (MRB), less APL 26, relocated from Dong Tam, and was escorted to an anchorage on the My Tho River 5 miles east-southwest of My Tho in order to provide close support for the impending operation.

'RAD 71 was unopposed as they beached their battalion at the first light on the banks of the Giao Hoa Canal one mile from the My Tho River. The riverine units continued to support the ground forces from the waterways as the troops ashore moved south on both banks toward the junction of the Giao Hoa Canal and the Bai Lai River — often referred to as ''crossroads''.

'At 08.43 the assault craft of RAD 92 with their troops came under a vicious ambush from an enemy force of unknown size about 4 miles northeast of Ben Tre. The devastating assault occurred on the Bai Lai River just as the boats were moving in toward the beach to land their troops and consisted of heavy rocket, recoilless rifle, automatic weapons and small arms fire. The land mass bordering the river at this point was a densely foliated jungle with coconut palm forest, thick undergrowth at the water's edge and the enemy fire came from heavily fortified and well-concealed bunkers within the maze. Despite the withering onslaught of intense enemy fire and the heavy casualties suffered, the riverine craft immediately delivered a barrage of cover fire at the attackers and landed their infantrymen. A violent firefight erupted. One company of troops landed directly in front of several enemy bunkers and remained pitted down in that precarious position for the rest of the day. Due to their proximity to the enemy fortification supporting fire could not be delivered on the bunkers.

'Five personnel were killed and more than sixty were wounded in the initial assault with the heavy fighting continuing throughout the morning. Two Navymen aboard monitor ''92-2'', Chief Boatswain's Mate Samuel C. CHAVOUS USN, the boat's captain, and Third Class Boatswain's Mate John D. WOODARD USN, the Coxwain, were killed and two others wounded in the firefight.

'Following the first two hours of heavy fighting, enemy resistance slackened off to steady harassment with machine gun and small arms fire. At 12.30 six sailors aboard monitor 91-3 were wounded when their craft patrolling on the Bai Lai River 500 yards west of the crossroads were attacked with rockets and automatic weapons, three of the wounded men were "medevaced" from the combat scene; one of them, Fireman Douglas G. MORTON, USN, died of wounds.

'As a result of the combat action on 4 April, twelve assault craft received various degrees of material damage. The most extensive damage was inflicted on A-91-2 and A-92-4. A total of six RPG-7 rockets impacted against the two boats, three of which were direct hits on the .50 calibre gun mounts. One monitor M-92-2, received a HEAT round through the opening between the 20 mm and .50 calibre gun mounts killing the boat captain and the coxswain.

'One ATC received an RPG-7 round through the bow ramp, which severed the ramp winch cable and wounded 30 Army personnel in the well deck. Another ATC was hit by an RPG-7 rocket amidships near the waterline. The rocket then triggered on the bar armour, penetrated the bulkhead and created a shrapnel effect inside the empty well deck.

'Sporadic contact with the fiercely resisting enemy continued throughout the first day and night. By the evening of 5 April, 35 Viet Cong had been killed and 2 prisoners were captured. One of the prisoners identified his unit as the Viet Cong 516th Provincial Mobile Battalion. Friendly losses at that time were 10 killed (3 USN, 5 USA, 1 ARVN and 1 Vietnamese interpreter), 119 wounded (36 USN, 81 USA, 2 USMC), and 2 Army men missing.

'On 6 April after two days of rigorous fighting the MRF had a day of relative calmness as they shifted the centre of operations from the Bai Lai River to a point 4 miles southeast of Ben Tre. Cumulative results for the three-day operation were 102 Viet Cong killed and 6 prisoners captured, while friendly forces had 33 killed (3 USN, 28 USA, 1 ARVN and 1 Vietnamese interpreter) and 152 wounded (36 USN, 81 USA, 2 USMC). The MRF units also destroyed 46 bunkers, captured 4 weapons and detained 25 Viet Cong suspects.

'During the afternoon of 7 April the infantrymen were backloaded by RADs 91 and 92 and returned to the MRB anchorage on the My Tho River about 5 miles east of My Tho, thereby terminating a very costly operation for the MRF.'

WINDING DOWN THE WAR
1968 – 73

In late 1968, the Johnson administration, convinced after the Tet Offensive of February and March and the follow-up attacks during the spring that the allied military struggle was not faring well and buffeted by growing domestic opposition to the American role, ordered the gradual withdrawal of US forces from Southeast Asia. The Vietnamization of the war was the cornerstone of American policy during the period 1968-73.

A new naval campaign was launched in October 1968 when the Navy was still at peak strength. SEALORDS (Southeast Asia Lake, Ocean, River, and Delta Strategy) programme was designed as a concerted effort by US Navy, South Vietnamese Navy, and allied ground forces to cut the enemy's supply lines from Cambodia and disrupt operations at the base areas deep in the Mekong Delta.

At that time the US Navy's Coastal Surveillance Force operated 81 Swift boats, 24 Coast Guard WPBs, and 39 other vessels. The River Patrol Force deployed 258 patrol and minesweeping boats. The 3,700 man Riverine Assault Force counted 184 monitors, transports, and other armoured craft and HAL 3 flew 25 armed helicopters. In addition, five SEAL platoons were available for operations in the Delta. Complementing the American naval contingent were the Vietnamese Navy's 655 ships, assault craft, patrol boats, and other vessels.

Two Navy OV-10 Bronco V/STOL aircraft of Light Attack Squadron Four (VAL-4) fly over a river near the Cambodian border in search of Viet Cong.

Right *Another Bronco from VAL-4 takes off to cover a PBR patrol operating on the waterways of the Cambodian border.*

Below *Strike assault boat (STAB) makes a high speed patrol near the Cambodian border, Operation 'Sealords', June 1970.*

The air component of SEALORDS was soon augmented by fifteen fixed-wing OV-10 Bronco aircraft of Light Attack Squadron (VAL) 4, activated in April 1969. The lethal Bronco assigned to the Marine Corps was flown by the 'Black Ponies' of Val 4. The aircraft was armed with between eight and sixteen Zuni rockets, nineteen 2.75 in rockets, four M-60 machine guns, and a 20 mm cannon.

Although continuing to function, 'Game Warden', 'Market Time' and the Riverine Assault Force (Task Force 117) operations were scaled down and their personnel and *matériel* increasingly devoted to SEALORDS. Task Force 115's PCFs carried out swift raids into enemy-held coastal waterways and assumed patrol responsibility for the Delta's large river. This freed the PBRs for operations along the previously uncontested smaller rivers and canals. These intrusions into former Viet Cong strongholds were possible only with the on-call support of naval aircraft and the heavily armed riverine assault craft.

The first phase of the SEALORDS campaign required the establishment of patrol 'barriers', often using electronic sensors, along the waterways paralleling the Cambodian border. In early November 1968, PBRs and riverine assault craft opened two canals between the Gulf of Thailand at Rach Gia and the Bassac River at Long Xuyen. South Vietnamese paramilitary ground troops then helped naval patrol units secure the transportation routes in this operational area soon named 'Search Turn'. Later in the month, Swift boats, PBRs, riverine assault craft, and Vietnamese naval vessels penetrated the Giang Thanh-Vinh Te canal system and established patrols along the waterway from Ha Thien in the gulf to Chau Doc on the upper Bassac. To reflect the Vietnamese contribution to the combined effort, the name of the operation was soon changed from 'Foul Deck' to 'Tren Hung Dao I'.

Then in December 1968, US naval forces pushed up the Tuan Co Dong and Vam Co Tay Rivers west of Saigon, against heavy enemy opposition, to cut infiltration routes from the 'Parrot's Beak' area of Cambodia. The 'Giant Slingshot' operation (so-called for the configuration of the two rivers) severely hampered communist resupply in the region near the capital and in the Plain of Reeds. Completing Phase I of the SEALORDS programme in January 1969, PBRs, assault support patrol boats (ASPB) and other river craft established patrol sectors along canals westward from the Vam Co Tay to the Mekong River in operation 'Barrier Reef'. Thus, by early 1969 a waterway interdiction barrier extended almost uninterrupted from Tay Minh northwest of Saigon to the Gulf of Thailand.

GLOSSARY

AGC Amphibious force flagship
AGF Miscellaneous flagship
AGMR Major communications relay ship
AGSS Auxiliary submarine
AH Hospital ship
AK-47 Chinese-made automatic rifle
AKA Amphibious cargo ship
AN Netlaying ship
APA Attack/Amphibious transport
APB Self-propelled barracks ship
APC Armoured Personnel Carrier (land)
APD Amphibious transport (small)
APL Barracks ship, non-self-propelled
APSS Amphibious transport submarine
ARG Amphibious Ready Group
ARL Landing craft repair ship
ASMS Advanced Surface Missile System
ASPB Assault Support Patrol Boat
ASROC Anti-Submarine Rocket
ATC Armoured Troop Carrier
ATC(H) ATC fitted with helicopter pad
AV Seaplane tender

B-40 Chinese-made rocket
BB Battleship

CA Heavy cruiser
CAG Heavy guided missile cruiser
CCB Command and communications/control boat
CCVP Landing craft, vehicle, personnel
CG Coastal Group
CG Missile cruiser
CGN Missile cruiser (nuclear)
CIDG Civilian Irregular Defence Group
CINCPAC Commander-in-Chief, Pacific
CINCPACFLT Commander-in-Chief, Pacific Fleet
CL Light cruiser
CLG Light missile cruiser
COMUMACV Commander US Military Assistance Command, Vietnam

CVA Attack carrier
CVAN Attack carrier (nuclear)
CVS Anti-submarine carrier
CVT Training carrier

DASH Drone Anti-Submarine Helicopter
DD Destroyer (gun-only)
DDG Missile destroyer
DE Destroyer (escort)
DE-AGDE Escort destroyer (gun-only)
DE-DER War-built escort ship
DEG Missile escort destroyer
DER Radar picket destroyer
Dinassauts *Division navales d'assaut* (naval assault divisions)
Dixie Station US Seventh Fleet afloat base in South China Sea, 11 deg. N. 110 deg. E — operational only in the early part of the Vietnam War
DL Frigate (gun-only)
DLG Missile frigate
DLGN Missile frigate (nuclear)

E8 Expendable riot-control gas grenade launcher.
ECM Electronic Counter-Measure
EOD Explosive Ordnance Disposal

FSB Fire Support Base

Game Warden US Navy (Task Force 116) operation designed to thwart Viet Cong use of inland waterways as supply and infiltration routes

HAL Helicopter light squadron
HMAS Her Majesty's Australian Ship

IUVU Mobile Inshore Undersea Surveillance Group 1, Western Pacific Detachment

JGS Joint General Staff

LCA Landing Craft, Assault
LCC Amphibious command ship
LCI Landing Craft, Infantry
LCM Landing Craft, Mechanized

LCPL Landing Craft, Personnel, Large
LCPR Landing Craft, Personnel, Ramped
LCT Landing Craft, Tank
LCU Landing Craft, Utility (a light lift craft)
LCVP Landing Craft, Vehicle or Personnel
LFR Inshore fire support ship (rocket-equipped)
LHA Amphibious assault ship
LKA Amphibious cargo ship
LPA Amphibious/Attack transport
LPD Dock-landing ship
LPH Amphibious assault ship
LPR Amphibious transport, small
LPSS Amphibious transport submarine
LSD Dock-landing ship
LSIL Landing Ship, Infantry, Large
LSM Landing Ship, Medium
LSMR Amphibious fire support ship (rocket-equipped)
LSSL Landing Ship, Support, Large
LST Landing Ship, Tank
LVT Organic tracked landing vehicle
LZ Landing Zone

M-16 Standard American automatic rifle
M-43 Soviet-made rifle firing intermediate 7.62 mm cartridges
M102 American-made 105-mm howitzer
MACV US Military Assistance Command, Vietnam
Market Time US Navy (Task Force 115) operation designed to seal the coast of South Vietnam against infiltration of enemy troops and supplies
MCS Mine countermeasures support ship
MDMAF Mekong Delta Mobile Afloat Force
MMD Fast minelayer
MMF Fleet minelayer
MON (Monitor) An armoured gunboat armed with 20- and 40-mm guns and 81-mm direct fire mortars
MRB Mobile Riverine Base
MRF Mobile Riverine Force

(Task Force 117)
MSB Minesweeping Boat
MSC Coastal minesweeper, non-magnetic
MSF Fleet minesweeper (war-built)
MSI Inshore minesweeper
MSL Minesweeping Launch
MSO Ocean minesweeper, non-magnetic
MSS Special minesweeper

NIOTIC Naval Inshore Operations Training Centre
NVA North Vietnam Army – Communist regulars

PACV Patrol Air Cushion Vehicle
PBR River Patrol Boat
PCF Inshore Patrol Craft (Swifts)
PG Patrol Gunboat
PHG Patrol Gunboat Hydrofoil
POL Petrol, Oil and Lubricants

RAG Riverine Assault Group
RIVERFLOTONE River flotilla one
RPD Chinese-made light machine gun
RPG Soviet rocket-propelled grenade
RPG 2,7 Soviet anti-tank

rockets
RSSZ Rung Sat Special Zone – an extensive mangrove swamp near Saigon used by the Viet Cong for base areas

SAMID Anti-missile integrated ship
'Sea Dragon' force Special US coastal bombardment group assigned to patrolling the North Vietnam coast
SEA LORDS The US Navy's Southeast Asia Lake, Ocean, River, Delta Strategy Operations
SEALs Navy sea-air-land commando teams
SKS Chinese-made carbine
SLF Special Landing Force
SPDMS (Basic) Point Defence Missile System
SSBN Fleet ballistic missile submarine
SSG Guided missile submarine
SST Training defence submarine
STAB SEAL Team Assault Boat

Task Force 76 US Seventh Fleet's attack carrier striking force
Task Force 77 US Seventh

Fleet's amphibious force
TF Task Force

VAL Marine light attack aircraft squadron
Viet Cong Communist guerrillas operation in South Vietnam, 1959–75
Viet Minh Forerunners of the NVA – raised in World War 2 to fight Japanese; fought against the French in the Indochina War, 1946–54

WPB US Coast Guard cutter
WHEC US Coast Guard High Endurance Cutter

X-craft Submersibles

Yankee Station US Seventh Fleet afloat base in South China Sea, 16 deg. N. 110 deg. E — operational throughout the Vietnam War
YD Floating crane
YFNB Large covered lighter
YLLC Salvage lift craft, light
YRBM Repair, Berthing and Messing barge
YRBML Repair, Berthing and Messing barge (large)
YTB Large harbour tug
YTL Small harbour tug
YTM Medium harbour tug

132

INDEX

133

Of further interest . . .

AIRCRAFT OF THE VIETNAM WAR

Perhaps because the Allied, and increasingly US-led, forces involved in the Vietnam war enjoyed almost complete air superiority for most of the lengthy conflict, it is often not realized that the opposing Communist forces also operated a variety of aircraft, though not to anything like the same extent. Virtually every aircraft of either side, and certainly every aircraft to have seen service in more than the most limited numbers, is listed with appropriate specifications in this fully illustrated but handy and reasonably priced reference work.

Bill Gunston has here identified and described not only the aircraft used by each side but also the particular marks and adaptations that were made to basic airframes for increased performance in the Vietnam conflict environment. *Includes colour photographs.*

VIETNAM HELICOPTER HANDBOOK

Although the value of the helicopter as a military aircraft was first appreciated during the Korean War, it was in the treacherous jungle and swampland of Vietnam that it later proved itself indispensable.

Described and illustrated here are all the helicopters that contributed to the crucial 'airmobility' concept which permitted essential troop movements, combat, and search and rescue operations to take place even in such an inhospitable environment. The text gives detailed specifications of each helicopter with development and deployment histories, and specific operations are vividly recounted.

Examining the complete background to the role of the helicopter in Vietnam, this is a useful illustrated guide for the aviation enthusiast and a fascinating study for the military historian. *Includes colour photographs.*